MW01140714

CONVERSATIONAL FRENCH:

QUICK AND EASY

BARBARA B. SALOOM

Copyright 1993 by Barbara B. Saloom
ISBN: 0-9627755-1-7
Published 1993 by Professor Barbara B. Saloom
Third Printing 1995

Also by Barbara B. Saloom
Converational Spanish: Quick and Easy , 1988. Seventh Printing 1994
ISBN: 0-9627755-0-9

Boxford, Massachusetts, Tel: 508-887-2581 Fax: 508-887-0752

To the many students who have helped me with their interest, enthusiasm, and questions as we worked together to learn to "get along" in French.

PREFACE

Conversational French books are available to students, but many of them presuppose some knowledge of French, some experience with another foreign language, or an adequate knowledge of grammar. Many of the books are addressed to secondary school students and the material is not pertinent to an adult. Some beginners are frightened and give up because the material seems too difficult and/or the subject matter inadequate.

Conversational French: Quick and Easy is presented to the adult or the college student who wants to attain a speaking knowledge of French with the stress more on communication and comprehension than on grammatical depth. It is useful to tourists, business people who travel to French-speaking countries, and those who want the enrichment and enjoyment of learning a foreign language.

This book accompanies a course that will be very useful to the student and still not intimidate or embarrass him with long grammatical terms; i.e., demonstrative adjectives are called "Ways to say 'this' or 'that';" possessive adjectives are called "Ways to explain possession;" conjugations are explained in terms of how we explain who is performing the action; etc. Every student speaks many times during each lesson, and mistakes in grammar are minimized if not entirely overlooked. Again, the main purpose of the book is for the student to speak and to understand the spoken word, even if imperfectly. He is encouraged to use motions or descriptions in vocabulary with which he is acquainted if he does not know the exact vocabulary; i.e., "facial tissues" could be "papier pour le nez" (paper for one's nose) or even "le Kleenex."

The general format of each lesson includes:

1. **Vocabulary:** to be repeated many times in class and memorized, partially by classroom repetition but also at home, aloud, if possible.

2. **Explanation:** an informal explanation, in layman's terms, of grammar.

3. **Culture:** some description of French customs so that the American will not make an inappropriate remark to a French-speaking person. It also includes helpful material for the tourist.

4. **Practice:** suggestions for impromptu dialogues and conversation. Grammatical exercises or explicit duplication of French for English is purposely avoided so that the student can "think in French" as much as possible in this short a course.

5. **Extra vocabulary:** Since a minimum of vocabulary which the student can use to make himself understood is offered in the first part of each lesson, extra vocabulary is presented at its end for enrichment.

With the use of this book, students will be speaking French to one another and to the teacher from the very first day of class. Emphasis is on repetition. Only the present tense is used in the first ten lessons. The future and a past tense are introduced in Lessons 11 through 15.

There are two forms for "you" in French, one used with close friends and relatives and one used with strangers or people in high positions. Since the student will probably be dealing with French people whom he does not know very well, the first ten chapters will use the formal "vous," and the informal "tu" will be introduced in Chapter 11.

The lessons are kept light and personal so that the student is relaxed and perhaps even entertained. Use of the first name is encouraged, regardless of age.

Dear Teacher,

This type of course is a joy to teach. You have the ideal situation: your students <u>want</u> to learn French. Undoubtedly, you have many ideas for the enrichment of the lessons. One that I have found to be meaningful to the adult student is the presentation of current events of France or French-speaking countries or areas. Students often like to participate by bringing in their own travel or current event articles or telling about something they have seen or heard on television or radio. Many like to share with the class their experiences with French people with whom they may work or whom they may have met abroad.

Any cultural material, such as music or souvenirs of France or French speaking countries brought to class by the teacher or students, adds color and interest to the course. A French guest speaker who talks to the class about his country can expect many diverse questions from adult students.

Try to keep the conversation going in class by coming prepared with a long list of questions. Students seem to enjoy current, local, personal, and silly questions, such as, "Comment s'appelle le président des Etats-Unis?", "Qu'est-ce qu'il y a dans votre réfrigérateur?" "Combien de bouches a Louise?"

An idea for a fun-type, as well as learning, experience is to form groups during class time, give each group a different specific situation, and have them prepare their own dialogues. For example, "Mother, father, and their child (may be from three to 30 years old!) are discussing plans for the day. They cannot seem to come to an agreement and finally look at the clock and decide that it is too late to do anything."

Enjoy your students and your course!

Dear Student,

You may have learned a language taught in a more traditional way. The approach taken in this book will be different, but it will enable you to learn French faster.

Most of the tools of the language are presented here, but some are not absolutely essential for your purpose, namely, "getting along in French." Such things as accent marks and punctuation, exact use of "the" or "a" or of the gender of a French noun appear in the "Explanation" section, but you will be understood even if you do not remember all of these grammatical points.

Some advice which may help you is to memorize diligently the "Vocabulary" section. Practicing aloud is more effective for the student whose aim is primarily to speak and understand the language. Some students find it helpful to bring a tape recorder to class, some make flash cards and carry them about with them to use in spare moments, some listen to French programs on television or radio. Perhaps you can use your French with a French-speaking person. Do whatever your situation permits to expose yourself as frequently as possible to the French language.

Bonne chance!

CONTENTS

Many thanks to my son, Ambassador Joseph A. Saloom, III for careful editing of all aspects of the manuscript and to my cousin, William A. J. Barnes for help in editing the English sections. Thanks also go to my dear friends, Jean-Pierre Gillard and Charles Fadel for their generous help with the French language and phraseology.

Bart Addante helped with the layout of the illustrations in the book. The illustrations and cover were done by Mark Mrvicin . Thanks go to both.

And much appreciation is extended to my husband, Dr. Joseph A. Saloom, for helping me with desk top publishing.

FRENCH PRONUNCIATION

If you have opted to take this French course, you are probably predisposed to enjoy it. Like English, French spelling does not help too much with pronunciation. The underlined group of words are all pronounced like an o: maill<u>ot</u>, styl<u>o</u>, cad<u>eau</u>. You have no trouble pronouncing th<u>ough</u>, thr<u>ough</u>, and en<u>ough</u> so don't be intimidated by French pronunciation. Listen carefully to your instructor and let go your inhibitions. Do your best and do not be discouraged. You know people with foreign accents, you understand their English, you may even find their accents quite charming (like the French person speaking English). After your instructor has pronounced a word, repeat it several times.

You will find that French words of more than one syllable have a fairly even rhythm caused by pronouncing each syllable in the same pitch with the same amount of stress:

    voici   allons   toujours   salut

In saying the vowel sounds, the jaw, lips, and tongue muscles are held in a more tense position than in English, making the sounds shorter and more precise.

You may want to write these sounds down in your own private phonetics. We are presenting a phonetic sound and the closest English sound, wherever possible. It is not necessary to know the meaning of the word example. Just pronounce the words and get a feeling for the sound of the language.

VOWELS

A   a   Short clipped a:

            la b<u>a</u>n<u>a</u>ne   p<u>a</u>tois
            English: pat

    ɑ   Lips are spread and held tense, pronounced in the back of the mouth:

            p<u>â</u>té   t<u>a</u>sse   p<u>a</u>tisserie
            English: calm

E   e   Lips in a smiling position and jaws held very steady:

entr<u>er</u>   ch<u>ez</u>   t<u>é</u>l<u>é</u>
English: gate, but shortened

ɛ   Start from the position of the e sound, but spread your mouth into a more open smile. Always keep your jaws steady:

b<u>ê</u>te   él<u>è</u>ve   pr<u>e</u>sque
English: pet

ə   A very small sound, something like "uh." Mouth is relaxed and sound made in back of mouth:

l<u>e</u>   pr<u>e</u>mier   m<u>e</u>nace
English: compose

NOTE: After me, le, je, ne the ə sound is frequently omitted:

Jel_ sais.	Je le sais.
Jen_ sais pas.	Je ne sais pas.
Quil_ voit?	Qui le voit?

I   i   Smile widely and tautly and say "me":

<u>i</u>l   Phil<u>i</u>ppe   l<u>i</u>re
English: seat

j   Like the y in "yes":

ca<u>hi</u>er   f<u>ill</u>e   somme<u>il</u>
English: layer

O   ø   Lips pursed, sound something like the little sound of ə but slightly stronger:

p<u>eu</u>   d<u>eu</u>x   nev<u>eu</u>

œ This sound is similar to the sound ø but the lips are more rounded, and the sound slightly more open:

coul<u>eu</u>r fl<u>eu</u>r m<u>eu</u>ble

o Lips more rounded and tense:

cad<u>eau</u> styl<u>o</u> m<u>ot</u>
English: go, but shortened

ɔ Lips less rounded and tense than o. Always followed by a pronounced consonant:

p<u>o</u>ste éc<u>o</u>le v<u>o</u>ler
English: call, but pronounced a little bit more forward in the mouth

U y A very different sound from any found in the English language. Round your lips as if to make an o sound but make an i sound instead:

voit<u>u</u>re t<u>u</u> <u>u</u>ne

u Lips pursed firmly and protruded:

r<u>ou</u>ge gen<u>ou</u> t<u>ou</u>t
English: moon

NASALS

The nasal vowels are a combination of a vowel and a nasal sound. It is not a voiced n but rather one that goes through the nose as one sound with the vowel: un bon vin blanc. Listen to the difference between the nasal vowel and the vowel plus an n or m:

Nasal	N pronounced
cousin	cousine
grand	grande
mon	Monet

ɑ̃   The ɑ sound in combination with the nasal:

enfant   Jean   temps
English: Hong Kong

ɛ̃   The ɛ sound in combination with the nasal:

matin   américain   voisin
English: bang

ɔ̃   The ɔ sound in combination with the nasal:

allons   bonbon   non

œ̃   The œ sound in combination with the nasal:
brun   aucun   lundi

CONSONANTS

Most consonants are pronounced like English ones. The following are exceptions:

h   Not pronounced:

homme   heureux   heure

ŋ   Pronounced like an n followed by a y:

agneau   soigner   vigne
English: canyon

r   The r is the most difficult sound for the foreigner. Try a slight gargle in the back of the throat, the back of the tongue not quite touching the roof of the mouth:

arriver   rose   soir

Usually the final consonant is not pronounced:

Je vais   ils vont   chez vous

Exceptions: words that end in c, l, and r: ɔ ʃ

avec parc mal il bonjour professeur

When a word ends in e, the preceding consonant is always pronounced:

Louis Louise port porte

w   The w sound is frequent in the French spelling oi:

moi trois soif François
English: swat

LIAISON

A consonant not normally pronounced at the end of a word is pronounced and joined with the following word when that word begins with a vowel. Final s or x are pronounced like a z:

Vous aimez vos amis.
Vous avez deux enfants.
On arrive en avion.
Mon oncle aime son appartement.

ELISION

Le, la, que, ce, je, ne, me, te are substituted by an apostrophe for the vowel when followed by another vowel:

l' homme
l' étudiante
Qu' est-ce qu'il dit?
Il ne m'aime pas.
C'est important.
Nous t'avons vu hier.
J' aime
Je n' aime pas

LESSON 1

PRESENTATION

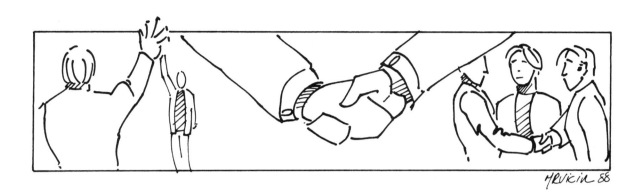

Bonjour, Marie.	Good day, Mary.
Bonsoir, monsieur Dupont.	Good evening, Mr. Dupont.
Bonne nuit, chérie (f), chéri (m).	Good night, dear.
Salut, mon vieux.	Hello, buddy. (m)
Salut, ma vieille.	Hello, pal. (f)
Comment allez-vous, monsieur?	How are you, sir?
Je vais très bien, merci.	I am very well, thank you.
Et vous?	And you?
Pas trop mal aujourd'hui.	Not too bad today.
Comment va Jean?	How is John?
Il va bien, merci.	He is well, thank you.
Comment vont Pierre et Anne?	How are Peter and Anne?
Ils vont bien.	They are well.
Comment allez-vous?	How are you?
Nous allons bien.	We are well.
Ça va?	How are things?
Bien, merci.	Fine, thanks.
Ça marche?	How is it going?
Ça marche.	Okay.
M. Johnson, je voudrais vous présenter M. Cartier.	Mr. Johnson, I would like to introduce Mr. Cartier.
Enchanté, monsieur.	Charmed, Sir.
Enchanté.	Charmed.

Ravi de vous connaître, Madame.	Delighted to meet you, Madame.
Je m'appelle Jean Dubois.	My name is John Dubois.
Je m'appelle Alice Caron.	My name is Alice Caron.
Comment s'appelle la dame?	What is the lady's name?
Elle s'appelle Anne Lavoisier.	Her name is Anne Lavoisier.
Comment s'appellent les enfants?	What are the children's names?
Ils s'appellent Edouard, Béatrice et Marie.	Their names are Edward, Beatrice, and Mary.
Adieu, Paul.	Good-bye, Paul.
Au revoir, Anne.	So long, Anne.
A bientôt, Edouard.	See you soon, Edward.
Salut, Claire.	So long, Claire.
A demain, Jean.	See you tomorrow, John.
A toute a l'heure, Marie.	See you soon, Mary.

EXPLANATION:

1. You have noticed in the above text four marks that you will not see in English:

présentation - acute accent
très - grave accent
François - cedilla
bientôt - circumflex

These marks sometimes change the pronunciation of a word:
The cedilla, found only under the letter "c," indicates that the "c" is to be pronounced like an "s".
The acute accent "é," found only over the letter "e," indicates that the sound is very close to the English "a" in "pay." The French sound is shorter than the English one and is produced by stretching the mouth into a tight smiling position. The grave accent "è" produces a sound very much like the "e" in the English word "get. The circumflex is more a matter of spelling and not of the utmost importance to us since we are taking an oral approach to the language.

2. Abbreviations:

monsieur	M.
madame	Mme
mademoiselle	Mlle

The abreviation is capitalized.

3. aller - to go (used with "bien" and "mal" to express how one
                  feels)

je vais	I go, am going, do go	nous allons	we go, etc.
(tu vas)	you (fam.) go, etc.	vous allez	you (formal sing. pl.) go, etc.
il va	he goes, is going, does go	ils vont	they (m) (m/f) go, are going, do go
elle va	she goes, etc.	elles vont	they (f) go , etc.

Each subject pronoun (I, you, he, she, we, they) has a certain form of the verb "to go" which must be used with it. Just as we would not say in English "I goes," we would not say in French "je va" but rather "je vais," if we meant "I go." These forms must be memorized as we learn new verbs. They come naturally to the native speaker, but, since we are not French, we resort to a function called "conjugation" to help us learn the verbs. You have seen above the conjugation of the verb "to go" or "aller." The "tu" form of "you" is in parentheses because we will not be using it for the first ten lessons of this book. There are two forms meaning "you" in French, "tu" used with close friends and relatives and "vous" used with strangers or people in high positions. Since you will probably be dealing with French people whom you do not know well, it will be safer for you to stick to the more formal "vous," which is used for the plural of "you" as well as the formal singular "you."

CULTURE :

French people are more apt to shake hands when meeting one another than Americans. In general, the woman extends her hand to the man, the older person to the younger, and the person in a higher position to the subordinate. Two women friends kiss one another on both cheeks and two men friends, who have not seen each other for some time, embrace and kiss one another on both cheeks. We should offer our hand when being introduced to a French person. The handshake is a firm but gentle pump rather than a continued shaking.

French people use the name of the person being addressed whenever possible (Bonsoir, monsieur Dupont). If they do not know the name, they use "madame," "mademoiselle," or "monsieur" (Comment allez-vous, monsieur?). A married woman or an unmarried woman of about 35 years of age is addressed as "Madame". "Mademoiselle" refers to a young woman.

PRACTICE:
USE A COMPLETE SENTENCE IN ALL THE PRACTICE DRILLS THROUGHOUT THE BOOK.

1. Each student turns to the student to his right and asks him in French what his name is. (Comment vous apelez-vouz?) The second student tells him his name, and this exercise is continued until everyone has spoken individually.

2. Each student turns to the student to his right and introduces to him the student to his left. Both students acknowledge the introduction. Keep this practice up until every student has participated.

3. Students greet one another by name and ask each other how they are or how someone else is. Try to vary the exchange by addressing two people or asking someone the name of others in the class.

EXTRA VOCABULARY:
Allons-y. Come on, let's go.
Bienvenu-e! Welcome!
comme ci, comme ça so-so
Mes amitiés a Marie. Greetings or regards to Mary.
garçon, le young boy, guy
jeune fille, la young girl
meilleur-e better
Salut! Bye!

Note: Abbreviations used are f - feminine, m - masculine, fam. - familiar, form. - formal, p - plural, s - singular

PARLONS

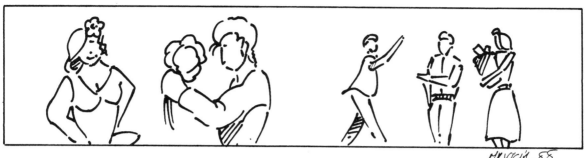

Oui	Yes
Non	No
S'il vous plaît	Please
Merci beaucoup	Thank you very much
De rien	You're welcome
Pardon	Pardon me
Excusez-moi	Excuse me
Je ne sais pas.	I don't know.
Je ne comprends pas.	I don't understand.
Répétez, s'il vous plaît.	Please repeat.
Je ne parle pas bien le français.	I don't speak French well.
Plus lentement, s'il vous plaît.	More slowly, please.
Comment dit-on _____	How does one say _____
en français?	in French?
Etes-vous français (e)?	Are you French (f)?
Non, je suis américain(e).	No, I am American(f).
Nous sommes canadiens(iennes).	We are Canadian(f).
Est-elle française?	Is she French?
Non, elle n'est pas française.	No, she is not French.
Sont-ils américains?	Are they American?
Non, ils ne sont pas américains.	No, they are not American.
Sont-elles canadiennes?	Are they Canadian?
Non, elles ne sont pas canadiennes.	No, they are not Canadians.

bon, bonne	good	grand-e	big
mauvais-e	bad	petit-e	small, little
beaucoup	a lot of, much	content-e	happy
un peu	a little	triste	sad
riche	rich	malade	sick

pauvre	poor	fatigué-e	tired
facile	easy	gentil, gentille	nice
difficile	difficult		

EXPLANATION:

1. Nationalities are written with a small letter:

> Etes-vous français?
> Non, je suis américain.

The word used to denote the people who speak the language is capitalized:

le Canadien	the Canadian
les Américains	the Americans

2. To make a word plural, the general rule is to add an "s." The pronunciation of the singular and the plural is the same.

3. To make a sentence negative, we put "ne" before the verb and "pas" after the verb:

> Non, elle n'est pas française.
> Non, ils ne sont pas américains.

Notice that "ne" becomes "n'" before a vowel. The apostrophe replaces the final vowel when the following word begins with a vowel:

l'Américain, l'Américaine	the American
l'enfant	the child
Est-ce qu'ils sont américains?	Are they Americans?

4. The most usual way to form a question is to invert the subject and verb and place a hyphen between the two:

> Etes-vous français?
> Sont-ils américains?

It is very simple to form a question if one learns the formula, "Est-ce que.......? " Simply put these words in front of the sentence:

Vous êtes français.	Est-ce que vous êtes français?
Ils sont américains.	Est-ce qu'ils sont américains?

5.   être - to be

je suis	I am	nous sommes	we are
(tu es)	you are	vous êtes	you are
il est	he is	ils sont	they are
elle est	she is	elles sont	they are

6. Gender plays a larger part in French than it does in English. Nouns are either masculine or feminine. Unless they obviously refer to a female ("la mère" - "the mother") or to a male ("le père" - the father), their gender must be memorized as the new vocabulary is presented. Masculine nouns use the word "le" and feminine nouns, "la" for the English word "the."

le livre	the book	la classe	the class
le crayon	the pencil	la table	the table

7. Number also has to be taken into consideration more often in French than in English. If the noun being described is plural, we usually add "s" to the descriptive words.

Il est grand.	He is big.	Ils sont grands.	They are big.
Henri est malade.	Henry is sick.	Nous sommes malades.	We are sick.

8. Both gender and number usually come into play when we are describing:

Il est content. (m,s)	He is happy
Ils sont contents. (m, p)	They are happy.
Elles sont contentes. (f,p)	They are happy.
Elle est fatiguée. (f,s)	She is tired.
Elles sont fatiguées. (f,p)	They are tired.

CULTURE:
English is recognized as the official international language today but its predecessor was French. The traveler will find French invaluable in widespread parts of the world. To name only a few examples: Canada - Quebec, the Caribbean - Martinique and Guadalupe, South America - French Guiana, the South Pacific - New Caledonia and Tahiti, and in Africa - Algeria, the Ivory Coast, and more than a dozen other African countries.

Most of the former French colonies still use French as their official language and some countries have French as one of their official languages, ie. French, German, and Italian are Switzerland's official languages and French and English are the official languages of Canada. In some former French colonies an older version of French is spoken (Cajuns of Louisiana) and, in some, such as Haiti, a mixture of French and local languages.

PRACTICE:
1. Quiz one another on the vocabulary learned up to now by asking, "Comment dit-on en français (English word or expression)?"

2. Ask each other questions using the vocabulary learned in Lessons 1 and 2.

Examples:
Ça marche? Comment va (name of student)? Comment s'appelle l'Américain? Etes-vous français(e)?

3. Using the nationalities and descriptive words you have learned up to now, ask one another questions.

Examples:
Est-il Français? Est-ce que Marie est gentille? Etes-vous malade? Est-ce que Jean et Paul sont riches?

EXTRA VOCABULARY:
Attendez un moment! Just a minute!
au contraire on the contrary
C'est pas vrai! You don't say!
en arrière backward, behind
favori, favorite favorite
fou, folle crazy, mad
important-e important
jeune young
joli-e pretty
laid-e ugly
merveilleux, merveilleuse marvelous
nouveau, nouvelle new
Pas possible! You don't say!
plus que jamais more than ever
populaire popular

Qui sait? Who knows?
Quoi de neuf? What's new?
sympathique pleasant
tout droit straight ahead
vieux, vieille old
Voyons! Let's see! Come on!

LESSON 3

LA FAMILLE

le mari	the husband
la femme	the wife
le père	the father
la mère	the mother
les parents	the parents, the relatives
le fils	the son
la fille	the daughter
le frère	the brother
la soeur	the sister
le grand-père	the grandfather
la grand-mère	the grandmother
les grands-parents	the grandparents

Parlez-vous français?	Do you speak French?
Oui, je parle français.	Yes, I speak French.
Et mes parents parlent français aussi.	And my parents also speak French.
Mais nous parlons anglais chez nous.	But we speak English at home.
Mon oncle parle anglais avec ma tante.	My uncle speaks English with my aunt.
Mon oncle et ma tante parlent un peu de français.	My uncle and aunt speak a little French.
il y a	there is, there are
Y a-t-il des Français à New York?	Are there French people in New York?
Oui, et il y a beaucoup de Franco-phones au Canada.	Yes, and there are many French-speaking people in Canada.

Est-ce qu'il y a

17

Il n'y a pas beaucoup de Français au Mexique.	There are not many French people in Mexico.
Avez-vous des enfants?	Do you have any children?
J'ai trois enfants.	I have three children.
Où sont les enfants?	Where are the children?
Ils visitent des amis.	They are visiting friends.
Pourquoi sont-ils en Californie?	Why are they in California?
Quand arrivez-vous à Montréal?	When are you arriving in Montreal?
Nous arrivons demain.	We are arriving tomorrow.
Comment voyagez-vous?	How are you traveling.
Je voyage en avion.	I am traveling by airplane.
Qui accompagne les grands-parents?	Who is accompanying the grand-parents?
Personne n'accompagne les grands-parents.	No one is accompanying the grandparents.
Qu'est-ce que les amis désirent?	What do the friends want?
Ils désirent manger tout de suite.	They want to eat right away.

un	one
deux	two
trois	three
quatre	four
cinq	five
six	six
sept	seven
huit	eight
neuf	nine
dix	ten

EXPLANATION:

1. The word "the" has four forms in French: le (masculine singular), la (feminine singular), les (plural), and l' (masculine or feminine singular before a vowel):

le fils	the son (masculine, singular)
la fille	the daughter (feminine, singular)
les hommes	the men (masculine, plural)
les femmes	the women (feminine, plural)
l'enfant	the child (before a vowel)

Notice that the forms "les" and "l'" do not indicate gender.

2. parler - to speak

je parle	I speak	nous parlons	we speak
		vous parlez	you speak
il parle	he speaks	ils parlent	they speak
elle parle	she speaks	elles parlent	they speak

We will not be presenting the "tu" form of the verbs until its use is explained in Chapter 11. "Vous" will serve as "you," singular and plural in our conversations. "Ils," "they" refers to males or males and females. "Elles," "they" refers to females.

In order to conjugate (See Lesson 1, Explanation 3) a verb that ends in "er," we remove the "er" ending and are left with the stem, "parl." To this stem we add "e" to express "I, he, she" speak, "ons" to mean "we" speak, "ez" to express "you" speak, and "ent" to express "they" speak. Any regular verb ending in "er" may be treated in this same manner.

3. Verbs that have a pattern like the above for conjugating are called "regular" verbs. French, like English, has irregular verbs as we have learned from our study of "aller" and "être." These verbs must be memorized. Irregular verbs that are used frequently will be presented in the first ten lessons.

4. avoir - to have

j'ai	I have	nous avons	we have
		vous avez	you have
il a	he has	ils ont	they have
elle a	she has	elles ont	they have

CULTURE:

French children enjoy spirited play with other children but are inclined to be quieter and more subdued with adults than American children.

Today, with advanced communications, customs are changing in France. Young people leave home to go where their work takes them. Small children stay at day-care centers as more mothers join the work force. The life style of the French people is very similar to our own.

PRACTICE:

1. Ask each other questions beginning with the question words: où, pourquoi, quand, comment, qui, qu'est-ce que

Examples:
Où est Jean? Pourquoi parlez-vous? Qui va à Mexique?

2 Use the "er" verbs presented in this lesson (parler, visiter, arriver, voyager, accompagner, désirer) with varied subjects.

Examples:
Marie désire parler. Je voyage à Paris. Nous arrivons à Quebec. Anne et Lorraine accompagnent aux grands-parents.

3. Prepare two questions, using the material in this lesson, to ask your classmates.

4. Count from one to ten.   Count from ten to one.

EXTRA VOCABULARY:
beau-fils, le   son-in-law
beau-frère, le   brother-in-law
beau-père, le   father-in-law
belle-fille, la   daughter-in-law
belle-mère, la   mother-in-law
belle-soeur, la   sister-in-law
Ça suffit!   That will do!
chat, le   cat
chien, le   dog
compagne de chambre, la   roommate (f)
compagnon de chambre, le   roommate (m-
couple, le   married couple
cousin, le   cousin (m)
cousine, la   cousin (f)
faché-e   angry
femme, la   woman
fier, fière   proud
gâté-e   spoiled
gens, les   people
homme, l'   man
voyage de noce, le   honeymoon
neveu, le   nephew
nièce, la   niece

oiseau, l' bird
personne, la (m,f) person
petit-fils, le grandson
petite-fille, la grandaughter
prendre une photo to take a snapshot
saluer to greet
stupide stupid, foolish
veuf, le widower
veuve, la widow

LESSON 4

L'HEURE ET LE TEMPS

Quelle heure est-il?
Il est une heure.
Il est une heure dix.
Il est quatre heures.
Il est sept heures cinq.
Il est huit heures moins vingt.
Il est deux heures et demie.
Il est une heure et quart.
Il est trois heures moins le quart.
A quelle heure arrivez-vous?
à neuf heures du matin
à trois heures de l'après-midi
à huit heures du soir

Il est midi.
Il est minuit.

Où vont les petites filles?
Elles vont à l'école le matin.
Je vais à la maison l'après-midi.
Il est de bonne heure.
Il est tard.

What time is it?
It is one o'clock.
It is ten after one.
It is four o'clock.
It is five after seven.
It is twenty of eight.
It is half past two.
It is quarter after one.
It is quarter of three.

At what time are you arriving?
at nine in the morning (A.M.)
at three in the afternoon (P.M.)
at eight o'clock in the evening (P.M.)

It is noon.
It is midnight.

Where are the little girls going?
They go to school in the morning.
I go home in the afternoon.
It is early.
It is late.

23

Quel temps fait-il aufourd'hui?		What is the weather like today?	

Il fait beau.	It is nice weather.
Il fait mauvais.	It is bad weather.
Il fait froid.	It is cold.
Il fait chaud.	It is hot.
Il fait frais.	It is cool.
Il pleut.	It is raining.
Il neige.	It is snowing.

Il finit le devoir.	He is finishing the homework.
Vous avez raison.	You are right.
Marie a tort.	Mary is wrong.
Nous avons peur.	We are afraid.
Les enfants ont sommeil.	The children are sleepy.
François a soif.	Francis is thirsty.
Nous avons chaud.	We are warm.
Vous avez froid.	You are cold.
Quel âge avez-vous?	How old are you?
J'ai vingt ans.	I am twenty years old.

onze	eleven	seize	sixteen
douze	twelve	dix-sept	seventeen
treize	thirteen	dix-huit	eighteen
quatorze	fourteen	dix-neuf	nineteen
quinze	fifteen	vingt	twenty

EXPLANATION:
1. To tell time, use the expression, "Il est," the number of hours, and the word "heure" for "It is one o'clock", and "heures" and the appropriate number for "It is two o'clock" and later.

Il est une heure.	It is one o'clock.
Il est cinq heures.	It is five o'clock.

To tell how many minutes after the hour it is, add the number of minutes:

Il est sept heures cinq.	It is five after seven.

To tell how many minutes before the hour it is, add the word "moins" (less) and the number of minutes.

> Il est huit heures moins vingt.   It is twenty minutes of eight.

"Half past" is "demie" and "quarter past" is "quart."

> Il est deux heures et demie.   It is half past two.
> Il est une heure et quart.   It is quarter after one.

The French translation for "quarter of" is "moins le quart."

> Il est six heures moins le quart.   It is quarter of six.

2.   finir - to finish

je finis	I finish	nous finissons	we finish
		vous finissez	you finish
il finit	he finishes	ils finissent	they finish
elle finit	she finishes	elles finissent	they finish

In order to conjugate a verb that ends in "ir," remove the "ir" ending and to the stem,"fin," add "is" to express "I finish," "it" to express "he" or "she finishes," "issons" to mean "we finish," "issez" for "you finish," and "issent" for "they finish."

After this lesson, the English meanings will be given only for the infinitive form. Infinitives, which are expressed in English with the word "to" and the verb (to speak, to finish, to take) have an ending of "er," "ir," and "re" in French (parler, finir, prendre).

3. This book deals mostly with present time. The French form for a present tense verb has three English translations:

Je vais.	I go, am going, do go.
Nous finissons.	We finish, are finishing.
Parlez-vous français?	Do you speak French? Are you speaking French?
Il voyage au Canada.	He travels to Canada. He is traveling to Canada. He does travel to Canada.

Note: "Do" plus the verb is used in English to translate a question. (Do you speak French?) When "do" is used for emphasis in English (I <u>do</u> know the answer.), a different construction is used in French.

CULTURE:

To express scheduled events (theater, trains, airplanes, the military, etc.), France uses the twenty-four hour system. One o'clock in the morning follows midnight and is "une heure." One o'clock in the afternoon is "treize heures," two o'clock, "quatorze heures," three o'clock, "quinze heures," etc. The twelve hour system is used in every day speech. "Une heure" could be one o'clock in the afternoon or early morning. If it is necessary to clarify which "one o'clock" they are referring to, they would say "une heure de l'après-midi" or "une heure du matin," just as Americans do.

The weather in France is somewhat more moderate than ours though it does vary throughout the country depending upon the geography. The climate of southern France is mild most of the year, the weather is cold and it snows in the mountain areas near Spain and Switzerland, and the coastal regions have a maritime climate.

We have all heard the expression, "Paris in the spring." The weather in Paris, indeed, is delightful in the spring. Many Parisians leave Paris in August because that is the hottest month in the year.

PRACTICE:

1. Quelle heure est-il? (Answer in a complete French sentence.)

a. 3:08 P.M.
b. 10:15 A.M.
c. 5:30
d. 20 of 6
e. 1:18

f. quarter of two
g. midnight
h. 4:15
i. noon
j. five of seven

2. A student calls upon another and asks, "Quel temps fait-il?" The student called upon answers with any weather expression, then calls upon another student who uses a different response. This continues until each student has responded.

3. Ask questions of other students using a verb from the conjugation that ends in "ir" (finir, choisir, grossir, maigrir, rougir).

Examples:
Finissez- vous le devoir?   Pourquoi rougit-elle?   Qui maigrit?

4. Ask questions of the other students using the "avoir" expressions.

Examples:
Qui a sommeil? Avez-vous raison? Combien d'ans a René?

5. Go around the class giving each other mathematical problems.

Examples:

Combien font trois et cinq?	How much are three and five?
Trois et cinq font huit.	Three and five are eight.
Combien font dix-neuf moins quatre?	How much are nineteen minus four?
Dix-neuf moins quatre font quinze.	Nineteen minus four are fifteen.

6. You now know how to greet each other, make introductions, take leave of one another, tell nationalities, discuss your family, describe people, tell what time it is and at what time you do a certain activity, what the weather is like, people's ages, etc. Form into groups of two or three, take ten or fifteen minutes to prepare a conversation, and then present your conversation to the class.

EXTRA VOCABULARY:
automne, l' (m)   autumn
C'est ça.   That's right.
calendrier, le   calender
ciel, le   the sky
climat, le   climate
d'abord   at first
date, la   date
en ce moment   right now
en même temps   at the same time
été, l' (m)   summer
fête, la   holiday
glace, la   ice
hiver, l' (m)   winter
jour ouvrable, le   work day
minute, la   minute
mouillé   wet
neige, la   snow
peu à peu   little by little
pluie, la   rain

plus tard   later
presque   almost
printemps, le   spring
réussir   to succeed
saison, la   season
sec, sèche   dry
second-e   second
souvent   often
suivant-e   following
tempête, la   storm
tonnerre, le   thunder
tous les jours   every day

LESSON 5

LES METIERS

Que faites-vous?	What kind of work do you do?
Je suis ingénieur.	I am an engineer.
Et vous, que faites-vous?	And what do <u>you</u> do?
Je suis mécanicien.	I am a mechanic.
Quelle est la profession de Gérard?	What is Gerard's profession?
Il est professeur.	He is a teacher. (or a professor)
Et mon cousin/ma cousine est secrétaire.	And my cousin is a secretary.
Notre frère est infirmier.	Our brother is a nurse.
Notre soeur est infirmière aussi.	Our sister is also a nurse.
Il faut que les médecins travaillent beaucoup.	Doctors have to work a lot.
Les ménagères travaillent à la maison.	Homemakers work at home.
Les étudiants et les professeurs travaillent à l'université.	Students and teachers work at the university.
Quelques avocats gagnent beaucoup d'argent.	Several lawyers earn a lot of money.
Son cousin est un charpentier très industrieux.	His (her) cousin is a very industrious carpenter.
Lundi, ils vont à la maison avec M. Gillard.	On Monday, they are going home with Mr. Gillard.
Les cuisiniers et les sommeliers travaillent dans un restaurant.	Cooks and wine stewards work in a restaurant.

Les coiffeurs et les coiffeuses travaillent dans un salon.	Barbers and hairdressers work in a barber shop (or hairdresser's).
Michel voudrait devenir architecte.	Michael wants to become an architect.

à	to, at
dans	in
de	of, from
avec	with

Elle perd son argent.	She is losing her money.
Ils descendent l'escalier.	They are coming down the stairs.
Je réponds à la lettre.	I am answering the letter.
Nous attendons nos amis.	We are waiting for our friends.

Quel jour sommes-nous?	What day is today?
Nous sommes:	Today is:

lundi	Monday	vendredi	Friday
mardi	Tuesday	samedi	Saturday
mercredi	Wednesday	dimanche	Sunday
jeudi	Thursday		

vingt et un	21	trente-deux	32
vingt-deux	22	quarante	40
vingt-trois	23	quarante et un	41
vingt-quatre,etc.	24	quarante-deux	42
trente	30	cinquante	50
trente et un	31	soixante	60

EXPLANATION:

1. The words for "a" and "an" in French are "un" before a masculine work and "une" before a feminine word:

un restaurant	a restaurant
une infirmière	a nurse

2. In telling one's occupation in French, we do not use the word "a" (un, une) unless the occupation is modified (described):

Je suis ingénieur.	I am an engineer.
Ma cousine est secrétaire.	My cousin is a secretary.

Son cousin est un charpentier très industrieux.	His (her) cousin is a very industrious carpenter.

3. Possession:

The words that express possession agree with the person or thing that is possessed. The forms may be masculine, feminine, or plural.

mon frère	my brother	notre frère	our brother
ma soeur	my sister	nos frères	our brothers
mes parents	my parents	votre frère	your brother
		vos frères	your brothers
son frère	his/her brother	leur frère	their brother
sa soeur	his/her sister	leurs frères	their brothers
ses parents	his/her parents		

4. The days of the week are written with a small letter. Use the word "le" with days of the week to express an habitual action:

Ils aiment aller au cinéma le samedi (les samedis).	They like to go to the movies on Saturday (Saturdays).

If no recurring action is indicated, simply use the day:

Ils vont chez M. LaPlante mardi.	They are going to Mr. LaPlante's house on Monday.

5.   vendre - to sell

je vends	nous vendons
	vous vendez
il vend	ils vendent
elle vend	elles vendent

To conjugate a verb that ends in "re," remove the "re" ending, and to the stem "vend," add "s" to say "I sell." There is no ending to express "he," "she sells". The plural endings are the same as those for the "er" conjugation, "ons," "ez," "ent."

6.   vouloir - to wish, want

je veux	nous voulons
	vous voulez
il veut	ils veulent
elle veut	elles veulent

7. Contrary to English usage, words used in a general sense, require the word "the" before them:

> Les médecins travaillent beaucoup.
> Les ménagères travaillent à la maison.

CULTURE:
The equal rights movement is going on in France just as it is in other countries. Some words denoting professions formerly practised only by men and now also engaged in by women have kept the masculine forms for both men and women (le médecin, l'ingénieur) and some have a new form (la conductrice).

France has had a Socialist type of government for the last decade and the people have been enjoying such benefits as four week vacations, national medical insurance, high minimum wages, family compensation for each child, etc. However, the Socialist government was voted out of office in 1993. Budget pressures will undoubtedly require that such benefits be curtailed.

The French calendar shows Monday as the first day of the week and is sometimes confusing to the American who is accustomed to seeing Sunday as the first day.

The two most popular spectator sports in France are soccer ("football" in French) and the "Tour de France," a long (2500 miles) and difficult (through mountainous areas) bicycle competition. Baseball is not popular among the French. Just as we have professional baseball, France has professional "football." The competition is very strong within the country and on the international field, stronger than baseball in the United States. Rugby is the second most popular sport and basketball, volleyball, tennis and skiing follow. French people also enjoy fishing, hunting, swimming, and card playing. Some older men play the old French game of "boules" which resembles bowling but is played outdoors using small metal balls.

PRACTICE:
1. Tell what you plan to do each day.

Examples:
Lundi je vais au restaurant. Mardi je vais au salon. Mercredi je travaille à l'école., etc.

2. Each student recites one consecutive number from one to sixty nine, in turn, first counting by one, then two, then three, then five, and then ten.

3. Ask questions of other students using a verb from the conjugation that ends in "re" (perdre, descendre, répondre à, attendre).

Examples:
Est-ce que vous perdez votre argent? Qu' est-ce qu'il répond?

4. Form into groups of two or three and take ten or fifteen minutes to prepare a conversation about your work. Use your imagination. You might like or not like your work. Perhaps you work in a different country. Maybe you work with a relative or friend. See if your fellow students show by their reaction that they understand what you are saying by injecting some humor into your dialogue.

EXTRA VOCABULARY:
acteur, l' (m)   actor
actrice, l' (f)   actress
affaires, les (f)   business
artiste, l' (m,f)   artist
astronaute, l' (m,f)   astronaut
au lieu de   instead of
bureau, le   office
célèbre   famous
client, le   client, customer (m)
cliente, la   client, customer (f)
compagnie, la   company
curé, le   priest
de temps en temps   from time to time
détective privé, le   private detective
diplomate, le,la   diplomat
directeur, le   manager
droit, le   right
échec, l' (m)   failure
emploi, l' (m)   job
employé-e, l' (m,f)   employee
enseigner   to teach
étudier   to study
faire une demande d'emploi   to apply for a job
habileté, l' (f)   skill, ability

homme d'affaires, l'   business man
Il faut   It is necessary.
journaliste, le   journalist
mériter   to deserve
on doit   one should, ought to
patron, le   boss
prix, le   prize
professeur, le (m,f)   professor
profession, la   profession
programmeur, le   programmeuse, la   computer programmer
psychologue, le, la   psychologist
renvoyer   to fire
salaire, le   salary
soldat, le   soldier

LA MAISON

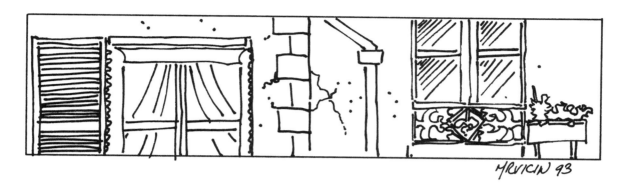

MRVICIN 93

Où habitez-vous?
J'habite un village en banlieue de Paris.
J'ai une grande maison: il y a beaucoup de pièces dans ma maison.
Il y a un salon, une salle à manger, une cuisine, deux salles de bain, et quatre chambres à coucher.
Il y a aussi un sous-sol.
La maison de mon grand-père est petite.
Nous mangeons le petit déjeuner et le déjeuner dans la cuisine, et le dîner dans la salle à manger.
Quelquefois nous déjeunons en plein air.
Nous avons une machine à laver et un réfrigérateur.
Nous avons très souvent de la visite.
Alors nous jouons au bridge et nous mangeons un petit quelque-chose avec des boissons gazeuses ou du vin.
Les petits jouent dans le jardin.

Where do you live?
I live in a town in the outskirts of Paris.
I have a big house: there are many rooms in my house.

There is a living room, a dining room, a kitchen, two bathrooms, and four bedrooms.

There is also a basement.
My grandfather's house is small.

We eat breakfast and lunch in the kitchen, and dinner in the dining room.
Sometimes we have lunch outside.
We have a washing machine and a refrigerator.
We very often have company.

Then we play bridge and have a little snack with some soda or wine.

The children play in the garden.

Quand nous n'avons pas de la visite, nous lisons des revues et des livres, nous payons des factures, nous travaillons dans le jardin ou nous faisons la sieste.

When we don't have company, we read magazines and books, we pay bills, we work in the garden, or we take a nap.

Nous nettoyons la maison chaque semaine.

We clean the house every week.

Notre maison se trouve sur la Rue Léon dans la petite ville de Cholet.

Our house is on Leon Street in the little town of Cholet.

Il y a une boutique à droite.

There is a shop to the right.

A gauche il y a une pharmacie.

There is a drugstore to the left.

C'est la pharmacie de M. Duval.

It is Mr. Duval's drugstore.

Il y a beaucoup de grandes routes dans ma ville.

There are many highways in my city.

Il y a des édifices hauts et des petites maisons.

There are tall buildings and small houses.

Nous avons une université et plusieurs églises et écoles.

We have a university and several churches and schools.

janvier	January	juillet	July
février	February	août	August
mars	March	septembre	September
avril	April	octobre	October
mai	May	novembre	November
juin	June	décembre	December

Quelle est la date?

What is the date?

C'est aujourd'hui le premier septembre.

Today is September 1.

C'est aujourd'hui le trois août.

Today is August 3.

EXPLANATION:

1. In French. the word "the" is used with meals:

> Nous mangeons le petit déjeuner et le déjeuner dans la cuisine et le dîner dans la salle à manger.

2. To express possession in French, the word "de" is used between the thing possessed and the possessor:

La maison de mon grand-père est petite.

My grandfather's house is small.

C'est la famille de M. LeBlanc.

It is Mr. LeBlanc's family.

3. The combination of the words "de" and "le" becomes "du," "de" and "les" becomes "des." "A" and "le" become "au" and "à " plus "les" become "aux." "A la" and "de la" do not change.

Nous jouons au bridge.	We play bridge.
C'est la maison du professeur.	It is the professor's house.

4. The word "some" and "any" are very often omitted in English, but they must be used in French:

Nous lisons des revues.	We read magazines.
Voulez-vous du vin?	Do you want wine?

5. Dates are formed by using the word "le," the number, and the month. For the first day of the month, we use "le premier" instead of "1."
Like days of the week, months are written with a small letter.

C'est aujourd'hui le premier mai.	Today is May 1.
C'est aujourd'hui le neuf décembre.	Today is December 9.

6   venir - to come

je viens	nous venons
	vous venez
il vient	ils viennent
elle vient	elles viennent

7.   pouvoir - can, to be able

je peux (puis)	nous pouvons
	vous pouvez
il peut	ils peuvent
elle peut	elles peuvent

The form "puis" is used in questions:

Puis-je aller au cinéma avec vous?	May (can) I go to the movies with you?

8. The word "on" is used frequently in French. It means "we," "they," "one" and "people." "On" is used with the same verb form as "il" or "elle."

On va chez Marie.	They (we) are going to Mary's house.
On parle français en Algérie.	People talk French in Algeria.
On doit voter.	One should vote.

CULTURE:

French people entertain family and close friends in their homes.
They are more apt to take business or social acquaintances to a restaurant. But if one is invited to a French home, it is a good idea to be exactly on time and to bring a gift. If bringing flowers, do not choose roses or chrysanthemums. French people love flowers. There are usually cut flowers on the table and plants and flowers on windowsills and attached to shutters. The guest should greet the host and hostess first and then the children. One always shakes hands upon arrival and departure. The host and hostess may say, "Faites comme chez vous." which means "Make yourself at home." (Do not take this literally!) Be ready for excellent food and conversation. When you like what you are eating be sure to tell the hostess. The meal will have taken a long time in preparation and serving it will require a great deal of thought on the part of the hostess. Another reason to be very punctual. When you sit down at the table, you say "Bon appétit, madame or monsieur" and before drinking your wine, you say, "A votre santé, " always followed by the "monsieur" or "madame." The answer is "Merci, monsieur and/or madame, à la votre." "Merci," when not followed by "beaucoup" or "bien" is often used to mean "No, thank you." At the table you might say "Merci" and shake your head in a "no" gesture if you do not want something offered.

If one is complimented in France, instead of saying "Thank you," one shrugs off the compliment and says something along the lines of,"Oh, not really." To say "Thank you" would make you seem vain regarding your accomplishment.

Table manners are different in France. We keep our hand in our lap as we eat. French people have arms (not elbows) leaning on the table. They do not change hands when cutting their meat. Except for bread, nothing is eaten with the hands. It is proper to use the bread to move the food onto the fork. Fresh fruit is peeled and cut up and then eaten with a fork.

The table setting is also a bit different from ours. Spoons and forks are placed with the eating section part downward, facing the table cloth. A knife and spoon are placed above the plate for paring, slicing and eating the fruit. To the right of these utensils is the wine glass and, to the left, the water glass.

Housing in France is varied: apartment, villa, attached house, summer home, boarding house. If there is a "concierge," he or she lives in a small apartment on the ground floor. (In the United States we would call this floor the first floor.) The concierge helps tenants to carry baggage or packages in or out of their rooms and lets them into the building at night.

PRACTICE:

1. Prepare two questions to ask other students, using a possessive.

Examples:
Comment va le fils de Mme. Emerie?   Qui a la revue de Marie?

2. Ask a question of another member of the class in which you use the forms of "de" which are not used in English.

Examples:
Avez-vous des amis?   Voulez-vous des hors d'oeuvres, Madame?

3. Quelle est la date? Answer in a complete French sentence.

a. March 30
b. August 4
c. May 1
d. January 2
e. November 29

f. December 15
g. February 20
h. September 10
i. June 11
j. April 18

4. How many rooms are there in your house or apartment? Name them.

5. Tell five activities that you can do around the house.

6. Describe your town or city.

39

EXTRA VOCABULARY:

à côté de   beside, near
apparement   apparently
appartement, l' (m)   apartment
armoire, l' (f)   closet
bois, le   woods
cafard, le   cockroach
chaise, la   chair
chambre, la   room
champ, le   field
confortable   comfortable
coudre   to sew
drap, le   sheet
écouter   to listen
ennuyer   to annoy
Entrez!   Come in!
faire la sieste   to take a nap
fauteuil, le   armchair
fenêtre, la   window
garage, le   garage
gratte-ciel, le   skyscraper
grille-pain, le   toaster
jouer aux cartes   to play cards
jouer du piano   to play the piano
large   wide
lit, le   bed
meubles, les (m)   furniture
miroir, le   mirror
moderne   modern
objet, l' (m)   article
oreiller, l' (m)   pillow
Ouf!   Phew!
palais, le   palace
paysage, le   landscape
serviette, la   towel, briefcase
sofa, le   sofa
souris, la   mouse
table, la   table
tapis, le   carpet

LESSON 7

UN VOYAGE

MRGVKIN 93

Ils aiment beaucoup leur voyage au Canada.	They like their trip to Canada a lot.
Est-ce que vous aimez les grands voyages?	Do you like long trips?
Voici votre passeport.	Here is your passport.
Je n'ai rien à déclarer.	I have nothing to declare.
Je voudrais encaisser ce chèque de voyage.	I would like to cash this traler's check.
Vous pouvez changer votre arggent dans cette banque.	You can change your money in this bank.
Le porteur dit, "Par ici, monsieur."	The porter says, "This way, Sir."
Cette valise est lourde.	That suitcase is heavy.
Ce taxi va très vite, n' est-ce pas?	This taxi is going very quickly, isn't it?
Je porte mes bagages de l'aéroport (m) à l'hôtel (m).	I am taking my luggage from the airport to the hotel.
Où est la gare?	Where is the railroad station?
A quelle heure le train pour Lyon part?	When does the train to Lyon depart?
Combien coûte un billet à Cannes?	How much does a ticket to Cannes cost?
Je voudrais un billet aller et retour pour Nice.	I would like a round trip ticket to Nice.
Voyager en première classe coûte plus cher qu'en deuxième.	Traveling first class costs more than second class.
Vraiment?	Really?

French	English	French	English
Où sont les toilettes?	Where are the toilets?		
Elles sont tout droit.	They are straight ahead.		
Elles sont à droite.	They are to the right.		
Elles sont à gauche.	They are to the left.		
Nous partons encore une fois sur la voie 12.	We are departing again on Track 12.		

Faites le plein, s'il vous plait. — Fill it up, please.
Avez-vous besoin de l'huile? — Do you need oil?
J'ai un permis de conduire. — I have a driver's license.
Je voudrais louer un auto. — I would like to rent a car.
Je sais très bien conduire. — I know how to drive very well.

Combien de kilomètres y a-t-il jusqu'à Québec? — How many kilometers is it to Quebec?
Puis-je garer ma voiture ici? — May I park my car here?
Nous cherchons une station-service. — We are looking for a gas station.

rien	nothing	quelque chose	something
personne	no one	quelqu'un	someone
jamais	never	toujours	always
ni	nor, neither	ou	or

soixante-dix	70	quatre-vingts	80
soixante et onze	71	quatre-vingt-un	81
soixante-douze	72	quatre-vingt-dix	90
quatre-vingt-dix-neuf	99		
cent	100		

le printemps	spring	l'automne (m)	fall
l'été (m)	summer	l'hiver (m)	winter

le jour	day	le mois	month
la semaine	week	l'année (f)	year

EXPLANATION:

1. The numbers 70 to 79 are formed by adding the numbers 10 to 19 to the word 60 (soixante):

soixante-dix	70	soixante-douze	72
soixante et onze	71	soixante-treize	73 etc.

The numbers 80 to 99 are formed by adding the numbers 1 to 19 to quatre-vingts (four twenties or 80):

quatre-vingts	80	quatre-vingt-dix	90
quatre-vingt-un	81	quatre-vingt-onze	91
quatre-vingt-deux	82	quatre-vingt-douze	92 etc.

cent 100

NOTE: The final "s" is used only with 80, "quatre-vingts."

2. Usually adjectives that describe a noun follow the noun:

J'aime les édifices hauts.	I love tall buildings.
La robe rouge est très jolie.	The red dress is very pretty.

Exceptions: Short frequently used adjectives such as "bon," "petit," "jeune," "cher" "vieux" usually precede the noun:

Mon cher ami arrive le samedi.	My dear friend is arriving on Saturday.
Notre maison se trouve dans un petit village.	Our house is in a small town.

In some instances the descriptive word has a different meaning according as they precede or follow the noun:

cher ami	dear friend	la pauvre femme	the poor (to be pitied) woman
chapeau cher	expensive hat		
un grand auteur	a great author	la femme pauvre	the poor (no money) woman
un auteur grand	a tall author		

Other adjectives which do not describe the nouns precede them:

mon passeport
ce chèque
première classe
chaque jour

3. "Je voudrais" is a softer way to make a request than "je veux" just as in English "I would like" is less demanding than "I want." Use "je voudrais" because it is more polite.

Je voudrais encaisser ce chèque de voyage.

4. The words for "this" and "these" and for "that" and "those" are the same:

ce (m)   cette(f)   ces (pl)   cet (m, sing)   before a vowel
                                        or mute "h"

Cette valise est lourde.	This (that) suitcase is heavy.
Ce taxi va très vite.	This (that) taxi goes very quickly.
Cet homme demeure à Paris.	This (that) man lives in Paris.
Ces valises sont lourdes.	These (those) suitcases are heavy.
Ces taxis vont très vite.	These (those) taxis go very quickly.
Ces hommes demeurent à Paris.	These (those) men live in Paris.

NOTE: Occasionally there may be some ambiguity in a sentence because these forms have two meanings. The ending -ci for something nearby and -là for something further away are added, as follows:
Ce billet-ci coûte moins cher que ce billet-là.
This ticket is less expensive than that ticket.

5. We learned in Lesson 2 that to make a sentence negative, we place "ne" before the verb and "pas" after the verb. The same form is used for the following negative expressions:

ne............rien	nothing
ne............jamais	never
ne............personne	no one
ne............que	only
ne............plus	no more

Nous n'avons rien.	We don't have anything.
Il ne vient jamais.	He never comes.
Elles ne voient personne.	They don't see anyone.
Vous n'avez qu'un cousin.	You have only one cousin.
Je ne vais plus à ce café.	I don't go to that café any more.

6.　　　voir - to see　　　　　　savoir - to know

je vois	nous voyons	je sais	nous savons
	vous voyez		vous savez
il voit	ils voient	il sait	ils savent
elle voit	elles voient	elle sait	elles savent

7. "Aimer" (to like, to love), "désirer" (to want, to desire), "vouloir" (to want), "pouvoir" (to be able to, can), when followed by another verb require the infinitive form of the second verb:

Nous aimons danser.	We love to dance.
Ils veulent (désirent) manger tout de suite.	They want to eat right away.
Je sais très bien conduire.	I know how to drive very well.
Vous pouvez changer votre argent dans cette banque.	You can change your money in this bank.

CULTURE:

France is a very popular country for tourists: more than 44 million visit each year. Many stay only in Paris, the capital and heart of France, which has something for everyone. It is a capital of fashion, dining, intellectual conversation, architecture, and romance. Among the many fascinating sights are the Latin Quarter, the Eiffel Tower, the Arch of Triumph, the Notre-Dame Cathedral, the Bois de Boulogne, the Louvre, one of the greatest museums in the world, outdoor cafés, smart shops, and incomparable restaurants. Many visit the sewers, made famous by Victor Hugo in Les Misérables. The bateaux-mouches sailing along the Seine River afford an excellent overall view of Paris.

Outside of Paris each region of France has its own personality, depending, to a large extent, upon the land. In the north central, for example, the land is chalky. This land, combined with the mild climate allow for the production of champagne. The abundance of rain in Normandy makes possible excellent grassland for cows. French cheeses such as camembert are produced here. The cities and towns of the east which border upon Germany have many Germanic influences: the Alsatian dialect, which is mostly German with some French words, the charming peasant cottages, and the food, which includes "choucroute" very much like the German "sauerkraut." In the west, the medieval abbey of Mont Saint-Michel stands high on an island. La Bretagne has kept its traditional language, "le Breton."

Places one may visit in central France are the home of Jeanne d'Arc and the many chateaux along the Loire, some of which present "sound and light" performances, dramatizing their history. The raw material for making porcelain found in Limoges has led the city to become famous for its porcelain production. In the southern part of France, there is a medieval city, "la Cité de Carcassonne" where one can browse around the castle and its buildings and visit some of its many towers. Many famous painters (Cézanne, Van Gogh, Matisse, Picasso) have chosen to live in Provence because of its bright colors. The coastal region of southwestern France is very different from Provence. It is cooler and thickly wooded with pine trees. Visitors to this area will want to see Lourdes where miraculous cures are said to occur.

If the purpose of your vacation is amusement rather than touring, France offers spectacular beaches for bathing and sunning, very high mountains in the Alps for skiing, and the picturesque countryside for hiking and relaxing. Night life, shopping, fashion, and dining are all excellent in France.

PRACTICE:

1. Prepare two questions to be answered in a complete sentence in the negative by your fellow students.

Examples:
Est-ce que le taxi est grand?   Non, le taxi est petit.
Est-ce que vous voyez cette femme?   Non, je ne vois personne.

2. Prepare a short dialogue on each of the following:

        a. at the airport
        b. at the train station
        c. at the gas station

3. Compose five French sentences using different forms of "this," "these," "that," and "those."

4. Describe the weather in the different seasons.

5. Go around the class giving one another arithmetic problems.

Examples:
Combien font soixante et vingt?   Combien font cent moins trente?

EXTRA VOCABULARY:

À la semaine prochaine. See you next week.
agence, l' (f) de voyage travel agency
appareil photo, l' (m) camera
après after
assurance, l' (f) insurance
avant before
Bon voyage! Have a good trip!
brochure touristique, la tourist booklet
carte, la map
climatisation, la air conditioning
confirmer to confirm
côte, la coast
coûter to cost
d'ailleurs besides
dangereux, se dangerous
devant in front of
faire du camping to camp
faire la valise to pack one's suitcase
faire un voyage to take a trip
gare, la station
hôtel, l' (m) hotel
Je crois que oui. I believe so.
par exemple for example
pendant during
place, la seat
réservation, la reservation
réserver to reserve
selon according to
touriste, le, la tourist
train, le train
valise, la suitcase
visa, le visa
voyage d' affaires, le business trip

LESSON 8

UN RESTAURANT

Mavidin 93

Avez-vous faim?	Are you hungry?
Oui, et j'ai soif aussi.	Yes, and I am also thirsty.
Allons au restaurant.	Let's go to the restaurant.
Quel restaurant préférez-vous?	Which restaurant do you prefer?
J'aime les restaurants français.	I like French restaurants.
Il y a un restaurant parisien à côté de la bibliothèque.	There is a Parisian restaurant next to the library.
S'il vous plaît, apportez-moi la carte.	Please bring me the menu.
Qu'est-ce que vous allez manger?	What are you going to eat?

le beurre	butter	la pomme de terre	potato
la confiture	jam	les pommes frites	fried potatoes, French fries
l'oeuf (m)	egg		
le jambon	ham	le riz	rice
le lard	bacon	les haricots (m)	beans
les cornflakes	cornflakes	l'hamburger (m)	hamburger
la crème	cream	le porc	pork
le pain	bread	le poulet	chicken
les petits pains	rolls	la saucisse	sausage
le gâteau	cake	le fromage	cheese
le pain grillé	toast	les légumes (m)	vegetables
le sandwich	sandwich	les légumes verts	greens
la soupe	soup	le fruit	fruit
la salade	salade	les oranges (f)	oranges
le sel	salt	les pommes (f)	apples
le poivre	pepper	les raisins (m)	grapes
la glace	ice cream	les bananes (f)	bananas

Bon appétit! — Good appetite!

Eh bien, j'aime beaucoup les croques-monsieurs. — Well, I like toasted ham and cheese sandwiches a lot.

Le coq au vin est un plat délicieux. — Coq au vin is a delicious dish.

Je n'aime pas les plats trop épicés. — I don't like highly spiced dishes.

Que voudriez-vous boire? — What would you like to drink?

l'eau (f)	water	le citron pressé	French lemonade
l'eau minérale (f)	mineral water	le chocolat	chocolate
le lait	milk	le vin	wine
le café	coffee	le vin blanc	white wine
le café noir	black coffee	le vin rouge	red wine
le thé	tea	le cocktail	cocktail
la boisson gazeuse	soda	la bière	beer
le jus d'orange	orange juice	l'apéritif (m)	aperitif
la citronnade	lemonade		

Santé! — To your health!

Qu'est-ce qu'il y a comme dessert? — What is there for dessert?

Est-ce que le service est compris? — Is the service charge included?

un pourboire pour le bon service — a tip for the good service

un verre	a glass	une fourchette	a fork
une bouteille	a bottle	un couteau	a knife
une tasse	a cup	une cuillère	a spoon
		une petite cuillère	a teaspoon

le petit déjeuner	breakfast	la nourriture	food
le déjeuner	lunch	les hors d'oeuvres	appetizers
le dîner	dinner	le casse-croûte	snack

More "avoir" expressions:

avoir honte	to be ashamed
avoir de la chance	to be lucky
avoir besoin de	to need
avoir mal	to hurt (feel bad)
avoir envie de	to want to

EXPLANATION:

1. Some interrogatives are:

Qui - who	Qui vient chez nous?	Who is coming to our house?
Que - what	Que mangez-vous?	What are you eating?

Quel - (m), quelle (f), quels (m,p) quelles (f,p) - which

Quel livre lisez-vous?	What book are you reading?
Quelle robe est la plus jolie?	What dress is the prettiest?
Quels garçons jouent au parc?	What boys are playing in the park?
Quelles jeunes filles vont à l'université?	What girls are going to the university?

"Which" is followed by a noun and agrees in gender and number with this noun.

2. "Cent" is one hundred: it is not preceded by "un."
To express numbers from 101 to 199, add 1 to 99 to the word "cent":

cent	100	cent trente	130
cent un	101	cent quatre-vingts	180

To express numbers above 199, follow the same pattern:

deux cents	200
deux cent un	201
six cents	600
six cent quarante	640
huit cents	800
huit cent quatre-vingts	880

mille	1000
deux mille	2000
neuf mille	9000

Notice that "mille" does not add an "s."

J'ai mille francs.	I have a thousand francs.
mille neuf cent quatre vingt-treize	1993
mille huit cent	1800

Years may also be expressed by using dix-neuf cent, dix-huit cent, etc.

dix-neuf cent soixante-deux	1962
dix-sept cent cinquante-trois	1753

3. Verbs ending in "cer" and "ger":   In order to keep the original sound of the infinitive stem ending, it is sometimes necessary to make a spelling change. A verb whose stem ends in "c" adds the cedilla before the "o" and a verb whose stem ends in "g" adds an "e" before the "o" of the "nous" forms:

Je commence	Nous commençons
Je mange	Nous mangeons

Other verbs of these types are:

annoncer - to announce
prononcer - to pronounce
nager - to swim
plonger - to dive

4. In Lesson 4, we learned the conjugation of the "ir" verbs. There is a second group of "ir" verbs:

sortir- to go out

je sors	nous sortons
	vous sortez
il sort	ils sortent
elle sort	elles sortent

Notice that the plural forms of these verbs have the same endings as those of the "er" verbs. For the singular, the last letter of the infinitive stem is dropped and the endings "s" and "t" are added. Other verbs of this type are:

partir - to leave
dormir - to sleep
servir - to serve, wait on
mentir - to lie

5. faire - to make, to do   dire - to say, to tell

je fais	nous faisons	je dis	nous disons
	vous faites		vous dites
il fait	ils font	il dit	ils disent
elle fait	elles font	elle dit	elles disent

CULTURE:

As communications and high technology appear throughout the world, many of the old customs have to change. And so the former three meals a day with the family together, including a two hour lunch are rare today in France. However, France is still noted for its emphasis on good food and its preparation.

French cooking is famous all over the world. France abounds in restaurants, many serving the food of their particular regions: bouillabaisse, a fish stew, from Marseille on the Mediterranean Sea: fondue, made of French cheeses from the Alps: la choucroûte, a Germanic dish made with cabbage, white wine, sausage, and ham, from Alsace, close neighbor of Germany. Mention of French specialties well known abroad must be made: cuisse de grenouille (frogs legs), coq au vin (chicken prepared with wine), quiche lorraine (cheese pie), escargots (snails), cassoulet (a casserole of vegetables, beans, and several kinds of meat), and crêpes (thin pancakes).

Some favorites of French people today are crudités (raw vegetables served as an appetizer), vol-au-vent (meat pie made of chicken or calf sweetbreads), a plate of various cheeses. Cheese is served before dessert.

Most French people drink mineral water.

Today, to get the waiter's attention, one raises his hand and calls "Monsieur" rather than the former "Garçon." A waitress should be called "Madame" or "Mademoiselle." A service charge is added to the bill but, if the service is very good, a small tip is in order.

The "Menu à prix fixe" is a complete meal including hors d'oeuvres, entrée (sometimes with salad), cheese, dessert, and quite often, coffee. It is less expensive than ordering "à la carte" and is a very good choice for the foreigner since it is usually the specialty of the restaurant and/or the specialty of the day.

There are many cafés in France, some with outdoor terraces where one can enjoy the fresh air and watch people pass by, while having coffee, wine, beer, fruit juice, etc. One can, but is not obliged to, have a sandwich or dessert. In small towns no one will ask you to leave or order anything else even if you spend a couple of hours in a café.

Tipping is done in more cases in France than in the United States so be sure to have a lot of change available. Many are given for the same services as ours are: airport porter, taxi driver, hotel porter, waiter, coat checker, barber or hairdresser, telegram deliverer. Some tipping would not occur to us: the matron in the toilet, the woman in the restaurant who is in charge of the telephone, the person who takes you to your seat in a theater, any museum or monument guide, anyone who serves you in a gas station and the mailman who brings you a letter or a package. Tipping can be very annoying but we must remember that, more often than not, the tip is a part of the income to the receiver, who has a very small income, in some cases, none.

PRACTICE:

1. Draw up a menu for a French restaurant using "francs" and "centimes" for the prices.

2. Make out a grocery list.

3. Give the following numbers in French:

a. 1980	f. 1492
b. 1864	g. 728
c. 679	h. 305
d. 1766	i. 114
e. 501	j. 1227

4. Prepare two questions using the question words "qui," "que" or one of the various forms of "quel" to ask other students.

Examples:
Que voudriez-vous pour le dessert? Quelle revue avez-vouz?

5. Ask a question of your classmates using one of the new "avoir" expressions (p. 50, avoir honte, etc.).

Examples:
Avez-vouz envie de voyager? Avez-vous besoin des livres français?

6. Form groups and prepare a dialogue on food and meals to present to your class. Perhaps two or three of you are going to a restaurant. You might be inviting a friend for lunch or dinner. You may be discussing a third person and his/her skill or lack of skill in

preparing certain dishes. Use your imagination for the situations, and use the vocabulary learned up to now.

EXTRA VOCABULARY:
appétit, l' (m)   appetite
bar, la   bar
bifteck, le   steak
café, le   café
calorie, la   calorie
créme caramel, la   caramel custard
cuire   to cook
dans un petit moment   in just a minute
goût, le   taste, flavor
goûter   to taste
grossir   to put on weight
hot dog, le hot dog
L'addition, (f) s'il vous plaît.   The bill, please.
maigrir   to slim down
oignon, l' (m)   onion
omelette, l' (f)   omelet
payer   to pay
Perrier cassis, le   blackcurrent soft drink
plat international, le   foreign dish
plus ou moins   more or less
poisson, le   fish
prix, le   price
propriétaire, le   owner
régime, le   diet
rosbif, le   roast beef
siècle, le   century
sucre, le   sugar
viande, la   meat
whisky, le   scotch whiskey

LESSON 9

FAIRE LES COURSES

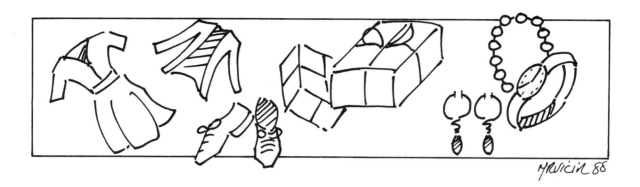

Prenons l'autobus au centre.	Let's go downtown by bus.
Moi, je préfère prendre le métro.	I prefer to take the subway.
Est-ce que le centre est loin?	Is the center far?
Non, le centre est à dix minutes de marche d'ici.	No, the center is a ten minute walk from here.
Nous pouvons y aller à pied.	We can walk there.
Bien	Okay
Y a-t-il beaucoup de boutiques là-bas?	Are there many shops there?
Qu'est-ce que vous voulez acheter?	What do you want to buy?
Il me faut acheter des vêtements (m) et je voudrais aussi acheter des cadeaux (m) pour mes amis aux Etats-Unis.	I have to buy clothes and also I would like to buy gifts for my friends in the United States.
Moi, aussi, je dois acheter quelques cadeaux.	I, too, should buy some gifts.
Jean achète des vêtements et Anne achète des bijoux (m).	John is buying clothing and Anne is buying jewelry.
Il achète un pantalon et elle achète une bague.	He is buying pants and she is buying a ring.
Il y a un magasin de vêtements au coin de cette rue-ci.	There is a clothing store on the corner of this street.
Vous désirez, monsieur?	May I help you, Sir?
Je cherche des souliers noirs.	I am looking for black shoes.
Quelle pointure faites-vous?	What size do you take?

Je chausse du cinq.	I take size five.		
Combien coûtent-ils?	How much do they cost?		
Cinq cent francs.	500 francs.		
Mon Dieu, ils sont très chers!	Goodness, they are very expensive!		
Pas de tout, ils sont bons marchés.	Not at all, they are inexpensive.		
Est-ce que je paye au vendeur?	Do I pay the shop assistant.		
Ou est-ce que je dois payer à la caisse?	Or should I pay at the cashier?		

la chemise	shirt	la jupe	skirt
le chapeau	hat	les bas	stockings
les chaussettes	socks	le pullover	sweater
le pantalon	pants	les chaussons (m)	slippers
la jaquette	jacket	la lingerie (f)	ladies underwear
les gants (m)	gloves		
les souliers	shoes	le mouchoir	handkerchief
le manteau	overcoat	le complet	suit
le maillot de bain	bathing suit	la robe	dress
		les sous-vêtements	underwear
le sac à main	handbag	le maquillage	make-up
les collants (m)	pantyhose	les lunettes	glasses
le soutien-gorge	bra		

l'image (f)	picture	le livre	book
le tableau	painting	le collier	necklace
l'appareil photo(m)	camera	les boucles d'oreilles	earrings

rouge	red	rose	pink
orangé-e	orange	pourpre	purple
jaune	yellow	brun-e	brown
vert-e	green	blanc, blanche	white
bleu-e	blue	noir-e	black
violet, ette	violet	gris-e	gray

EXPLANATION:

1. Il faut + infinitive means it is necessary, one must:

Il faut manger pour vivre.	It is necessary (one must) eat to live.
Il faut étudier chaque jour.	It is necessary (one must) study every day.

"Il faut" is used to express absolute necessity.

2. Devoir + infinitive means should or ought to:

je dois	nous devons
	vous devez
il doit	ils doivent
elle doit	elles doivent

Je dois aider Maman à faire le ménage.	I should (ought to) help Mom do the housework.
Nous devons aller à l'église tous les dimanches.	We should (ought to) go to church every Sunday.

"Devoir" is used to express an obligation.

3. We have learned the subject pronouns (je, (tu), il, elle, nous, vous, ils, elles). There is another group of pronouns which are used to emphasize the above subject pronouns. These pronouns may appear at the beginning or at the end of the sentence. They are as follows:

moi - me	nous - us
	vous - you
lui - him	eux - them (m, m and f)
elle - her	elles - them (f)

Moi, je préfère prendre le métro.	I prefer to take the subway.
Lui, il va à pied.	He's walking.
Ils vont à la maison, eux?	Are they going home?

These pronouns are also used after "chez," at the home of and "avec," with:

Nous allons chez eux.	We are going to their home.
Ils viennent chez moi.	They are coming to my house

J'étudie avec lui.	I am studying with him.
Marie travaillent avec elles.	Mary is working with them.

4. To express a command, use the verb form that ends in "ez":

Parlez plus lentement!	Speak more slowly!
Mangez le dîner!	Eat dinner!
Ecrivez une lettre!	Write a letter!
Allez à l'école!	Go to school!

These forms may also be used in the negative, placing "ne" before the verb and "pas" after the verb:

Ne parlez pas lentement!	Do not speak slowly!
Ne mangez pas le dîner!	Don't eat dinner!

5. For the expression "let us," use the verb form that ends in "ons":

Regardons le livre.	Let's look at the book.
Mangeons les croissants.	Let's eat the crescent rolls.
N'écrivons pas des lettres.	Let's not write letters.

6.   écrire - to write   lire - to read

écrire		lire	
j'écris	nous écrivons	je lis	nous lisons
	vous écrivez		vous lisez
il écrit	ils écrivent	il lit	ils lisent
elle écrit	elles écrivent	elle lit	elles lisent

CULTURE:

France has the full gamut of stores just as we do: the family-owned small shop, the boutique, the chain store, the large department store, the mall, and the huge discount store. In the center of small towns there are small shops which close, as so many did some years ago, between noon and 2:00 P.M. One greets the clerk when entering "Bonjour, madame, monsieur, mademoiselle" and, upon leaving, says "Au revoir," again using the title.
There are outdoor food markets where farmers set up stalls several times a week to sell local garden produce, piglets, chickens, meat, or fish, whatever that particular area of the country has to offer. You might find some kinds of meat that are not familiar to you: rabbit, calf's head, pigeon, horse. There are many other things in the

outdoor market such as furniture, linens, knick-knacks, and clothing. The kiosks, colorful stands on the sidewalks, sell newspapers, souvenirs, magazines, paperback books, cigarettes, and candy.

PRACTICE:
1. Ask one another, "Qu'est-ce qu'il faut faire en ville?"

2. Ask one another the colors of clothing or objects in the classroom.

Examples:
De quelle couleur est le sac à main de _____?
(someone in the class) De quelle couleur est le pantalon de
_____?

3. Ask a question of your classmates requesting them to use the (disjunctive) pronouns learned in this lesson.

Example:
Avec qui allez-vous au café? Chez qui étudiez-vous?

4. Play store. One person can be the shopkeeper and one or more others the customer(s). You might like to bring clothing or other items to class for this activity.

5. Practice the command form by telling your neighbor to do something. He, in turn, can show that he understands by performing the action required.

Example:
Ecrivez avec mon stylo.

EXTRA VOCABULARY:
annonce, l' (f)   advertisement
argent, l' (m)   silver, money
au dessus de   on, over
en dessous   under
baguette, la   long slim loaf of French bread
béret, le   beret
boucherie, la   butcher shop
boulangerie, la   bakery shop
C'est dommage.   It's too bad.
cravate, la   tie

crayon, le pencil
cuir, le leather
d'accord right, agreed
dépenser to spend
derrière behind
épicerie, l' (f) grocery store
grand magasin, le department store
imperméable, l' (m) raincoat
marchander to bargain
or, l' (m) gold
parfumerie, la perfume shop
porter to wear
poupée, la doll
pyjama, le pajamas
stylo, le pen
vendre to sell
vente, la sale
vers toward

LE CORPS HUMAIN

Je suis malade: j'ai mal a la tête.	I am sick: I have a headache.
Je me sens faible.	I feel weak.
J'ai mal au ventre.	I have a stomach ache.
Je suis enceinte.	I am pregnant.
A quelle heure est-ce que le médecin arrive?	At what time does the doctor arrive?
J'ai besoin de comprimés ou de médicaments (m).	I need pills or medecine.
Je suis allergique à la pénicilline.	I am allergic to penicillin.
Le médecin demande, "Où est-ce que vous avez mal?	The doctor asks, "Where does it hurt you?
Les dents me font mal; où y a-t-il un dentiste?	My teeth hurt; where is there a dentist?
Pouvez-vous préparer cette ordonnance pour moi?	Can you fill this prescription for me?
Il me faut aller en ville pour acheter des médicaments.	I have to go downtown to buy some medecine.
Il n'y a pas beaucoup de médicaments chez moi.	There's not much medecine at home.
Je demande de l'aspirine (f) à la pharmacie.	I ask for aspirin at the drugstore.

les cheveux (m)	hair	le doigt	finger
les yeux (m)	eyes	le bras	arm
le nez	nose	le derrière	buttocks
la bouche	mouth	la jambe	leg
la main	hand	les pieds	feet

le visage	face	le sein	bosom
la ceinture	waist	la poitrine	chest

J'ai les cheveux châtains. I have brown hair.
Papa a un grand nez. Dad has a big nose.

l'appendice (m)	appendix	l'injection	injection
la constipation	constipation	la fièvre	fever
l'insomnie (f)	insomnia	la toux	cough
les crampes (f)	cramps	l'insolation	sunstroke
le diabète	diabetes	le vomissement	vomiting
une fausse couche	miscarriage	le préservatif	condom
la diarrhée	diarrhea	le rhume	cold
le sparadrap	adhesive tape	l'iode (m)	iodine
le laxatif	laxative	la serviette hygiénique	sanitary pad
le thermomètre	thermometer	le tampon	tampon
un avortement	abortion	le SIDA	AIDS

Je voudrais que vous me: I would like you to:

fassiez les ongles. do my nails
coupiez les cheveux cut my hair
rasiez give me a shave
fassiez un shampooing give me a shampoo and
et mise en plis set
teigniez les cheveux de tint my hair the same
la même couleur color

Où y a-t-il une blanchisserie? Where is there a laundry?
Où y a-t-il un téléphone? Where is there a telephone?
Je voudrais téléphoner à ma I would like to call my wife
femme (mon mari, mon petit (my husband, my boyfriend,
ami, ma petite amie). my girlfriend).
S'il vous plaît, est-ce que vous Please dial for me.
feriez un numéro pour moi.
Je suis étranger (étrangère). I am a foreigner.
Qui est à l'appareil? Who is calling?
L'Hotel Paris, j'écoute. Hotel Paris, may I help you?
Quel est le prix de location d'une How much does it cost to rent
voiture pour une semaine? a car for a week?
Allô Hello (answer to a telephone call)

Je voudrais un film en couleur
  pour cet appareil.

I'd like a color film for this
camera.

EXPLANATION:

1. In French, the possessive (mon, son, votre, leur, etc.) is seldom used with parts of the body. The word for "the" is used:

J'ai les cheveux châtains.	I have brown hair.
Il a les yeux bleus.	He has blue eyes.

2. Some French verbs do not require a preposition where English verbs do:

Nous regardons le soleil.	We are looking at the sun.
Il demande son argent.	He asks for his money.
Vous habitez une jolie maison.	You live in a pretty house.
Ils cherchent un restaurant français.	They are looking for a French restaurant.
On paye les vêtements ici.	One pays for the clothing here.

3. On the other hand, some French verbs require a preposition where English verbs do not:

Nous jouons au basketball.	We play basketball.
Patrice et René entrent dans une boîte de nuit.	Patricia and René are entering a night club.
André répond à notre question.	Andrew answers our question.
Il oublie souvent de faire son travail.	He often forgets to do his work.
Essayons d' arriver à l'heure.	Let us try to arrive on time.

4. We have learned the expression "il faut" - it is necessary, one must. In order to make this expression refer to a person or persons, insert the following pronouns between "il" and "faut":

me	me	nous	us
		vous	you
lui	him, her	leur	them (m, f)

Il me faut aller chez ma tante.	I have to go to my aunt's house.
Il leur faut faire les devoirs.	They must do their homework.

5.

mettre - to put

je mets	nous mettons
	vous mettez
il met	ils mettent
elle met	elles mettent

CULTURE:

French people have a very animated way of speaking. They use their bodies a great deal when they speak. Not only do they use their mouths and facial muscles more than most English-speaking people do, but they also use their eyes, hands, their whole stance to emphasize their words. The following are just a few of the gestures used:

1. So-So - Both hands are open with the thumbs extended as the hands rotate from side to side.
2. Terrific! Great! - The thumb is raised and the other fingers bent under.
3. Who cares? I could care less. - Shoulders are held upward, hands lowered with palms facing outward while the person blows air through his mouth.
4. I don't know! - The corners of the mouth drop, the eyebrows are raised, arms raised with the palms of both hands facing the person spoken to.
5. That's enough! That's it! - Criss-cross your hands in front of you and move them several times outward.
6. It is worthless! - The thumb and pointer make a circle in front of an eye. This circle represents a zero.
7. I've had it up to here! I've had enough. Hand placed like a salute at the very top of the forehead.
8. I could do that with both hands tied behind my back! - Thumb and forefinger placed under nostrils. (Indicates that something is so easy, one can do it even with two fingers in the nose.)
9. How awful! Face shows fear or disbelief, eyebrows are raised, mouth is open, and a hand is in front of the mouth, palm facing outward.
10. You missed your chance! - Palm down, the hand moves from right to left under the nose. (It was right under your nose and you didn't take advantage of it.)

PRACTICE:

1. Ask two questions of your classmates about the body.

Examples:
Où se trouve le nez? Combien de doigts avez-vous?

2. One student is the doctor, another the patient. Prepare a dialogue for this situation.

3. A student asks another to do something for him. The student addressed shows by motions that he understands the request.

Examples:
S'il vous plaît, donnez-moi un médicament. Je voudrais que vous me rasiez.

4. Ask questions requiring the use of "il faut" of your classmates.

Examples:
Qu'est-ce qu'il vous faut faire? Qu'est-ce qu'il me faut faire?

5. Demonstrate one of the French gestures for your classmates to interpret.

EXTRA VOCABULARY:
accident, l' (m)   accident
Ah, mon Dieu!   Oh, my goodness!
Attention!   Watch out!
Au secours!   Help!
blessure, la   wound, injury
bracelet, le   bracelet
brosse à dents, la   toothbrush
cas urgent, le   emergency
coeur, le   heart
collier, le   necklace
dentifrice, le   tooth paste
en bonne santé   healthy
estimer   estimate, gauge
être humain, l'   human being
exercice, l' (m)   exercise
faible   weak
faire une promenade   to go for a walk

genou, le   knee
hôpital, l' (m)   hospital
Je suis désolé.   I am so sorry.
maladie, la   illness, sickness
malheureusement   unfortunately
marcher   to walk
Moi, non plus.   Nor I.
montre-bracelet, la   wrist watch
muscle, le   muscle
Oh, c'est affreux!   Oh, it's awful!
papier hygiénique, le   toilet tissue
Quel dommage!   What a shame! What a pity!
respirer   to breathe
risque, le   risk
santé, la   health
sauver (la vie)   to save (a life)
savon, le   soap
sieste, la   nap
symptôme, le   symptom

LESSON 11

LE BUREAU DE POSTE ET LA BANQUE

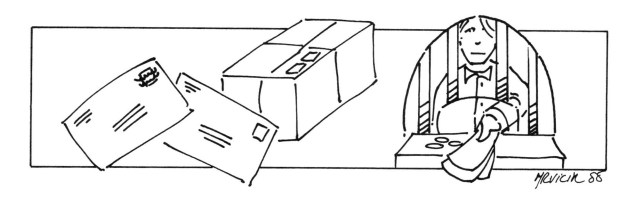

Hé, Antoine! Où vas-tu?

Hey, Anthony, where are you going?

Je vais au bureau de poste pour acheter des timbres (m).

I am going to the post office to buy some stamps.

Est-ce qu'il te faut aussi acheter une carte postale?

Do you have to buy a post card, too?

Je voudrais écrire une lettre à ma petite amie.

I want to write a letter to my girlfriend.

Je vais acheter du papier et des enveloppes (f).

I am going to buy some paper and envelopes.

Tu vas mettre ta lettre à la poste, n'est-ce pas?

You are going to mail your letter, aren't you?

Bien sûr!

Of course.

Peut-être que oui.

Maybe so.

Peut-être que non.

Maybe not.

Quels sont les tarifs postaux pour la Martinique?

How much is the postage to Martinique?

Tu ne dois pas envoyer de l'argent mais plutôt un mandat-postal ou un chèque.

You should not send money but rather a money order or a check.

Le facteur vient tous les jours.

The mailman comes every day.

Si tu emploies la poste aérienne, ta lettre va arriver bien plus tôt.

If you use air mail, your letter will arrive much sooner.

Nous envoyons toujours nos lettres par avion.

We always send our letters air mail.

Dieu merci! Je viens de recevoir un chèque des Etats-Unis.	Thank Heaven! I have just received a check from the United States.
Est-ce que tu vas encaisser le chèque à la banque?	Are you going to cash the check in the bank?
Il faut signer le chèque en dossier.	It is necessary to sign the check on the back.
Quels billets voulez-vous, Monsieur?	What denomination bills do you want, Sir?
Cent dollars en billets de cent francs et quatre-vingt en billets de cinquante francs, s'il vous plaît.	One hundred dollars in 100 franc bills and eighty in fifty franc bills, please.
Quel est le taux de change actuel?	What is the current rate of exchange?
Aujourd'hui le dollar vaut quatre francs.	Today the dollar if worth four francs.

EXPLANATION:

1. There is a future tense in French just as there is in English, "je parlerai," "I shall speak," etc. but it is simpler to use the word "aller" plus an infinitive to express time in the future:

> Est-ce que tu vas toucher le chèque à la banque?
> Tu vas mettre la lettre à la poste, n'est-ce pas?

As in English the present tense is often used to express future time:

Travailles-tu le lundi prochain?   Are you working next Monday?

2. The expression "n'est-ce pas?" at the end of a statement turns the statement into a question and can be translated as "isn't it," "aren't you," "doesn't he," "right?":

Tu vas mettre la lettre à la poste, n'est-ce pas?	You are going to mail the the letter, aren't you?
Cette leçon est très facile, n'est-ce pas?	This lesson is very easy , isn't it?
Jean écrit beaucoup de lettres, n'est-ce pas?	John writes a lot of letters, doesn't he?

3. The easiest way to ask a question in French is by the tone of one's voice. The voice goes up at the last part of the declarative sentence:

Tu viens demain?   Are you coming tomorrow?
Vous mangez à huit heures?   Are you eating at 8 o'clock?

We have learned to invert subject and verb to form a question:

Etes-vous heureux?   Are you happy?
Travaillent-ils à Paris?   Do they work in Paris?

If the il/elle form of the verb does not end in "t" or "d," the letter "t" is inserted:

     A-t-il sommeil?   Is he sleepy?
     Travaille-t-il en France?   Does he work in France?

We have already learned the following interrogative words:

où	where	comment	how
pourquoi	why	qui	who
quand	when	qu'est-ce que	what
combien de	how many	quel, quelle, quels, quelles	which, what

"Quoi" - "what" is used alone or after a preposition:

Quoi! Tu as une nouvelle Citroën!   What! You have a new Citroën?
De quoi avez-vous besoin?   What do you need?
A quoi est-ce qu'il pense?   What's he thinking about?

4. Up to now, we have used the formal form of "you" ("vous"). The form used among relatives and friends in the singular is "tu." The plural is always "vous," familiar or formal. For the "tu" form, add "s" to the "je" form for the -er verbs. For -ir and -re verbs, the "je" and "tu" forms are alike:

          je parle   tu parles
          je finis   tu finis
          je vends   tu vends

For the irregular verbs presented in Lessons 1 through 10, the "tu" forms are as follows:

aller	tu vas	savoir	tu sais
être	tu es	faire	tu fais
avoir	tu as	dire	tu dis
vouloir	tu veux	écrire	tu écris
venir	tu viens	lire	tu lis
pouvoir	tu peux	devoir	tu dois
voir	tu vois	mettre	tu mets
prendre	tu prends		

Où vas-tu?

Tu ne dois pas envoyer de l'argent.

NOTE: Forms end in "s" or "x."

To express a familiar command, use the familiar form ("tu") of the verb. "Er" verbs drop the final "s":

Parle!	Speak!
Sors!	Leave!
Descends!	Come down!
Viens!	Come!

NOTE: See Lesson 9 for formal commands.

5.

prendre - to take

je prends	nous prenons
tu prends	vous prenez
il prend	ils prennent
elle prend	elles prennent

CULTURE:

You will be spending francs and centimes in France. There are 20, 50, 100, 200, and 500 franc bills and coins go from five centimes to ten francs. You can find the exchange rate at your hotel, in a bank, or in the newspaper. It is best to change your American money at a bank that changes money because the rates are better than those offered at your hotel. You will have to show your passport for this service.

The use of "tu" and "vous" can be tricky for the foreigner. Youngsters always use "tu" with one another and "vous" with adults who are not family members. The use of "tu" can be offensive if used inappropriately. Use "vous" to be safe. The French person will take the initiative and you can follow his usage. Sometimes friends will ask each other if they may use the "tu" form.

PRACTICE:
1. Ask your fellow students one question having to do with the post office and one, the bank.

Examples:
Est-ce que vous achetez des timbres à l'hotel ou au bureau de poste?
Avez-vous signé le chèque?

2. One person plays the part of a postal clerk (employé-e des postes) and another the customer (le client). The customer asks two questions of the clerk and the clerk answers.

3. One person plays the part of the bank teller (caissier, ière) and another the customer. The customer asks two questions of the teller and the teller responds.

4. Using the familiar command form, tell someone to perform some action. The student answers the command in pantomime to show that he understands.

Examples:
Achète un manteau!   Ecris une lettre!

5. Form into groups and prepare conversations to present to the class involving friends who are on a "tu" basis. Subject matter should combine expressions learned in this lesson and those learned in Lesson 7, "Un Voyage ."

EXTRA VOCABULARY:
à propos   by the way
adresse, l' (f)   address
annonce, l' (f)   advertisement
billet, le   bill (money)
C'est tout.   That's all.
Ça dépend.   It depends.

calculatrice, la calculator
chèque de voyage, le traveler's check
code postal, le "zip" code
correct-e correct
déposer to deposit
emprunt, l' (m) the loan
emprunter to borrow
intérêt, l' (m) interest
mettre de coté to save (money)
montant, le amount
occupé-e busy
ouvrir un compte to open an account
pièce, la coin
poli-e polite
pourcentage, le percentage
prêter to lend
problème, le problem
remplir to fill out (a form)
rendre to return (give back)
retirer to withdraw
revenu, le income
témoin, le witness
traduire translate
tutoyer to use the familiar form of "you"
vite quickly
vol, le theft
voler to rob, to fly
volontiers gladly
vousvoyer to use the formal form of "you"

LESSON 12

LES FETES

MRUICIN 93

Félicitations!	Congratulations!
Bon Anniversaire!	Happy birthday!
Joyeux Noël!	Merry Christmas!
Bonne Année!	Happy New Year!

Faisons une fête.
Ils invitent leurs amis favoris.
Qui apporte de la champagne?
Paul, achète de la bière, s'il te plaît.
Ils prennent du vin rouge et du vin blanc.
Nous allons au supermarché à midi.
Il faut avoir de la musique.
Qui sait jouer de la guitare?

Raoul a beaucoup de compact disques.
Cette troupe sait jouer du rock très bein.
Dansons!
Nous allons servir du popcorn, des pommes chips, et des sandwiches.
A minuit nous nous faisons les adieux.

Let's have a party.
They invite their best friends.
Who is bringing champagne?
Paul, please buy beer.
They are having red wine and white wine.
We are going to the supermarket at noon.
We must have music.
Who knows how to play the guitar?
Ralph has a lot of CD's.

This group knows how to play rock very well.
Let's dance!
We are going to serve popcorn, potato chips, and sandwiches.

At midnight we say good-bye to one another.

Demain nous allons célébrer notre Fête Nationale, le quatorze juillet.	Tomorrow we are going to celebrate our National Holiday, the 14th of July.
Je me lève de bonne heure parce que je voudrais tout voir.	I get up early because I want to see everything.
Nous nous lavons la figure et nous nous peignons.	We wash our faces and we comb our hair.
Ensuite, nous sortons.	Then, we go out.
Les gens s'amusent beaucoup aux feux d'artifice.	The people have a very good time at the fireworks.
Ils retournent chez eux en voiture, à pied, en autobus, ou en train.	They return home by car, on foot, by bus, or by train.

EXPLANATION:

1. Unlike English, some French verbs require a short pronoun before the conjugated form of the verb. The infinitive of these verbs is preceded by "se" (se lever, se peigner).

Je me lève de bonne heure.
Nous nous peignons.

A chart for the conjugation of "se laver," "to wash up" follows:

je me lave	nous nous lavons
tu te laves	vous vous lavez
il se lave	ils se lavent
elle se lave	elles se lavent

Some common verbs of this type:

se coucher	to go to bed	s'amuser	to have a good time
se fâcher	to get angry	se laver	to wash up
s'apeller	to be named	se peigner	to comb one's hair
s'asseoir	to sit down	se lever	to get up

"S'asseoir" is very irregular:

je m'assieds	nous nous asseyons
tu t'assieds	vous vous asseyez
il s'assied	ils s'asseyent
elle s'assied	elles s'asseyent

NOTE: In the case of the previous examples, the person who performs the action is the same one as the person who receives the action. We are really saying: I put myself to bed, I make myself angry, I call myself, I seat myself, I amuse myself, I wash myself, I comb myself, I lift myself up, etc.

2. "Nous nous lavons la figure" is expressed in English as "We wash our faces." We use the singular "la figure" in French because each one of us has only one face. If the sentence were "We wash our hands," the French translation would be "Nous nous lavons les mains." "Les mains" is plural because we have two hands.

3. "Jouer" to play is used to mean 1. simply "to play," 2. to play a game and 3. to play a musical instrument:

>   1. Les enfants <u>jouent</u> dans le parc.
>   2. Nous aimons <u>jouer au basketball.</u>
>   Ils <u>jouent au bridge</u>.
>   3. Qui sait <u>jouer du piano</u>?

4. Some describing words are very different in the masculine and feminine:

Masc. Sing.	Masc. Pl.	Fem. Sing.	Fem.Pl.
beau (beautiful)	beaux	belle	belles
nouveau (new)	nouveaux	nouvelle	nouvelles
fou (foolish)	fous	folle	folles
vieux (old)	vieux	vieille	vieilles

> Lui, il n'est pas fou: mais, elle, elle est folle.
> <u>He</u>'s not crazy, but <u>she</u> is crazy.
> Cette robe-ci est nouvelle mais ce complet-là est vieux.
> This dress is new but that suit is old.

NOTE: "Vieux" has the same form in the singular and the plural.

CULTURE:
Most holidays are to celebrate a Catholic holy day, such as Christmas, Easter or a Saint's Day. Other religious holidays are observed with scarcely any religious significance attached.
Le quatorze juillet is France's National Holiday which celebrates the taking of the Bastille Prison and the beginning of the French

Revolution in 1789. Flags are displayed, there is a military parade, fireworks, and dances are held in the streets.

A typical fair would include rides, games, refreshments, and amusements. It could last as long as a week.

Mardi Gras begins on Ash Wednesday. There is a huge celebration in both the French city of Nice and the American city of New Orleans with enormous parades, highly imaginative costumes, and many happy and ingenious amusements. The Festival of Avignon is an annual summer festival of theater, modern, classical and street art, dance, and puppet shows--anything to do with the performing arts.

Parks are used more often in Paris and Montreal than they are in the United States. The Bois de Boulogne in Paris is spectacular: beautiful gardens, lakes, and waterfalls, a race course, a Shakespeare theater, a zoo, bicycle paths, bridle paths, and more. Many of the parks in France are small but afford city people an opportunity to stroll around and see the greenery and look at the people.

The gardens at Les Tuileries and Luxembourg are beautifully laid out and display many beds of flowers surrounded by pebbled walks.

Family celebrations, such as, birthdays and anniversaries, are sometimes observed in the home with a party. French people celebrate the date of the birth of the saints for whom they are named, as well as their own birthdays.

PRACTICE:

1. Use two of the verbs listed in Explanation 1. in a sentence or a question.

Examples:
Est-ce que tu t'amuses chez ton ami? Où s'asseyent-ils?

2. Prepare two questions about a party or celebration to ask of your fellow students.

Examples:
Quelle est la date de ta fête national? Qui achète la bière?

3. Greet a person with one of the expressions presented at the very beginning of this lesson and follow your greeting with a question or statement.

4. In groups of two or three, prepare a conversation on planning a party, using dates, location, perhaps some vocabulary from Lesson 9 (Faire les Courses), and the vocabulary of this lesson.

EXTRA VOCABULARY:
Allons donc.   Come on now. Really?
amusant-e   entertaining
bruit, le   noise
causer   to chat
costume, le   costume
crier   to shout
d'ordinaire   ordinarily
défilé, le   parade
excellent-e   excellent
gâteau, le   cake
intéressant-e   interesting
intolérable   really bad
invitation, 1 (f)   invitation
inviter   to invite
luxueux-se   luxurious
mariage, le   wedding
masque, le   mask
orchestre, l' (m)   band
rhum, le   rum
sans doute   no doubt, doubtless
soirée dansante, la   dance
surpris-e   surprised
Très bonne idée.   That's a fine idea.
typique   typical
verre de champagne, le   glass of champagne

LE SUPERMARCHE ET LE MARCHE
EN PLEIN AIR

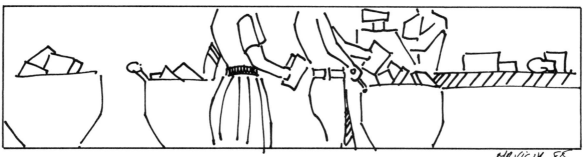

Nous avons autant d'argent que vous.

We have as much money as you.

Et donc, nous allons acheter autant de provisions que vous.

And therefore we are going to buy as many groceries as you.

Où est-ce qu'il y a un supermarché?

Where is there a supermarket?

Jean achète plus de viande que de légume.

John buys more meat than vegetables.

Son ami achète moins de thé que de café.

His friend buys less tea than coffee.

Vous désirez, Madame?

May I help you, Madame?

Je voudrais une boîte de petits-pois.

I would like a can of peas.

Et avec ça, Madame?

Anything else, Madame?

Est-ce que le poisson est frais aujourd'hui?

Is the fish fresh today?

C'est très frais, même plus frais que hier.

It's very fresh, even fresher than yesterday.

Et les légumes verts?

And the green vegetables?

Ils sont aussi frais que les autres légumes.

They are as fresh as the other vegetables.

Les deux ont été récemment cueillis au jardin.

Both are freshly picked from the garden.

Le gâteau est plus délicieux que le croissant.

The cake is more delicious than the crescent roll.

Est-ce que les noix coûtent plus cher que les fruits?

Do nuts cost more than fruit?

Est-ce que Madame Lapointe a payé la facture?

Has Mrs. Lapointe paid the bill?

Je n'ai accompagné personne au supermarché.

I haven't gone to the supermarket with anyone.

Bien, mais qui a vu Vincent au supermarché?

Okay, but who has seen Vincent at the supermarket?

Qui sait?

Who knows?

Ici on peut acheter un peu de tout.

Here one can buy a little of everything.

Oui, il y a de la nourriture, des vêtements, des assiettes, des tableaux, des jouets, des livres, et beaucoup d'autres choses.

Yes, there is food, clothing, dishes, pictures, toys, books, and many other things.

Dans le marché, on marchande pour baisser le prix.

In the market, one bargains to bargains to lower the price.

Quel dommage! On ne peut pas essayer les vêtements parce que nous sommes dehors.

What a pity! One cannot try on the clothing because because we are outdoors.

Combien d'argent as-tu dans le sac à main (la poche, le porte-feuille)?

How much money do you have in your handbag, (pocket, wallet)?

Seulement sept francs.

Only seven francs.

Eh, bien, nous pouvons au moins acheter une parapluie.

Okay, at least we can buy an umbrella.

Regarde là-bas, il y a un panneau qui dit "Ici on parle anglais."

Look, over there, there is a sign that says "English is spoken here."

Magnifique!

Great!

EXPLANATION:

1. In French, comparisons of equality:

    a. "as much, as many <u>noun</u> as" are expressed with "autant de <u>noun</u> que":

Nous avons autant d'argent que vous.

We have as much money as you.

Marie a autant de robes que sa soeur.

Mary has as many dresses as her sister.

b. "as <u>descriptive word</u> as" becomes in French "aussi <u>descriptive word</u> que":

Ils sont aussi frais que les autres légumes.	They are as fresh as the other vegetables.
Elles sont aussi intelligentes que leurs frères.	They are as intelligent as their brothers.

Notice that "frais" and "intelligentes" agree with the word that they are describing "ils" and "elles."

2. Comparisons of inequality:

a. "more, less <u>noun</u> than" are translated into "plus de, moins de <u>noun</u> que":

Jean achète plus de viande que de légume.	John is buying more meat than vegetables.
Son ami achète moins de thé que de café.	His friend buys less tea than coffee.

b. "more, less <u>adjective</u> than" is "plus, moins <u>adjective</u> que":

Le gâteau est plus délicieux que le croissant.	The cake is more delicious than than the crescent roll.
Le pain est moins cher que la viande.	Bread is less expensive than meat.

3. There are many past tenses in French but, in this course, we will "get along" with the most commonly used one. It is formed like one of the English past tenses: a form of "have" and a past participle (attended, served). The French "to have" is "avoir" and the past participle is formed by dropping the "r" of the infinitive for -er and -ir verbs and by substituting "u" for the -re ending verbs. The acute accent is used over the "e" in the past participle (parlé , mangé):

-er verbs	parler	parlé	spoken
	manger	mangé	eaten
-ir verbs	finir	fini	finished
	servir	servi	served
-re verbs	vendre	vendu	sold
	attendre	attendu	waited

NOTE: In Lesson 15 we will be studying the verbs (usually of coming and going) that require "être" as the helping verb.

The following shows the conjugation of the past tense that we will be using:

j'ai parlé	I spoke, have spoken
tu as parlé	you spoke, have spoken
il a parlé	he spoke, has spoken
elle a parlé	she spoke, has spoken
nous avons parlé	we spoke, have spoken
vous avez parlé	you spoke, have spoken
ils ont parlé	they spoke, have spoken
elles ont parlé	they spoke, have spoken

Like English , French has some irregular past participles:

faire	fait	made, done
prendre	pris	taken
mettre	mis	put
avoir	eu	had
être	été	been
voir	vu	seen

4. "y" and "en"

"y" is used to replace expressions of location and is translated by "there." It precedes the verb:

Nous allons à Paris.	We are going to Paris.
Nous y allons.	We are going there.
Le crayon est sur la table.	The pencil is on the table.
Le crayon y est.	The pencil is there.
Ils entrent dans la maison.	They are entering the house.
Ils y entrent.	They are entering there.

"en" usually means "some" or "any". It also prededes the verb:

J'ai mangé du pain.	I ate some bread.
J'en ai mangé.	I ate some (of it).
Anne a peu d'amis.	Anne has few friends.
Anne en a peu.	Anne has few (of them).
Ils ne prennent pas de lait.	They are not having any milk.
Ils n'en prennent pas.	They are not having any.

NOTE: "Y" and "en" are presented so that you will recognize them if you hear them. You can "get along" without having to use them.

CULTURE:
Canada is a bilingual country, English and French. More than 80% of the inhabitants of the province of Quebec are French-speaking. Quebec City is the capital of this province, but Montreal is the largest city and the second-largest French-speaking city in the world; Paris being the first. The cities have modern skyscrapers in commercial centers but they also have small, old, picturesque districts that are very charming and well worth visiting.

Like Spanish in the United States, French in Canada has been influenced by the English vocabulary and has many words of American origin. In some rural areas, people still speak a "patois," a provincial dialect, that may be a relic of the sixteenth century French spoken by Canada's discoverers. This patois cannot be understood by the tourist. Some of the French vocabulary in Canada that may not appear in Parisian French owes its development to the essentially different environment of Canadian French people. They needed words to describe the fauna and flora of a cold climate and their life and attitudes that have resulted from this environmental difference.

French pronunciation in Canada is somewhat different from that of France but not different enough to cause major difficulty in comprehension.

For the American tourist, Quebec City and Montreal offer a great opportunity to use French without the intimidation of not being understood or not understanding. Almost every Canadian can speak at least some English.

A French-speaking area that is very different from Canada is the far away island of Tahiti, located in the South Pacific. Here people have a delightful joie de vivre. French and Tahitian are the national languages and not much English is heard. Although the people have been influenced by the French, they still maintain many of their own traditional customs. Time is not important and Tahitians are against living by the clock. The typical food in rural areas is fish, sweet potatoes, breadfruit, taro, and potatoes. Almost all the people are a combination of Tahitian, Chinese, American, and European.

Tahiti is a blend of volcanic peaks and lush tropical forests, with white sandy beaches on one side of the island and black sandy beaches on the other side. Flowers and trees are abundant. The climate year round is warm.

Those who have visited Tahiti come back home planning for their next trip there. The warm, vivacious people, the weather, the easy pace of life, the natural beauty and color, dancing, and in its capital Papeete, French restaurants.......what more could one want?

PRACTICE:
1. Compose a sentence using a comparison of equality and one using a comparison of inequality.

Examples:
Pierre et Marianne sont aussi sympathiques que Jean et Brigitte. La voiture rouge est plus petite que la voiture noire.

2. Ask two questions of your fellow students using the past tense learned in this lesson.

Examples:
As- tu écrit beaucoup de lettres? Qui a vu Thérèse?

3. In groups of two or three, compose a conversation which occurs in a supermarket or an outdoor market. Try to provide variety by bringing in vocabulary learned in former lessons.

EXTRA VOCABULARY:
aider to help
balance, la scales
chercher to look for
comptoir, le counter
de temps en temps from time to time
demain tomorrow
doux, ce sweet
encore une fois again
faire la queue to stand on line
livre, la pound
long, ue long
lourd-e heavy
nécessaire necessary
net, te clean
paquet, le package
par ici around here

pas du tout   not at all
plein-e   full
plusieurs   several
qualité, la   quality
sale   dirty
tout le monde   everybody
utile   useful

LESSON 14

L'AEROPORT

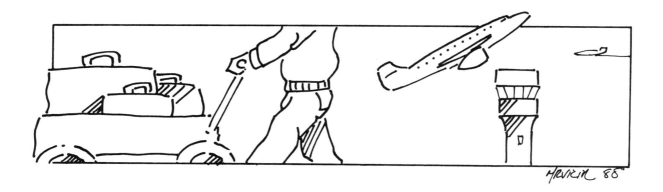

Jean et sa femme sont à l'aéroport.	John and his wife are at the the airport.
Les deux veulent aller à l'étranger.	Both want to go abroad.
Marie a peur de voler.	Mary is afraid of flying.
Mais on n'y peut rien: pour aller à la Côte d'Ivoire, il faut aller par avion.	But there's nothing anyone can do about it: in order to go to the Ivory coast, one must fly.
Ils achètent les billets.	They buy the tickets.
Ils sont très chers parce que la Côte d'Ivoire est très loin des Etats-Unis.	They are very expensive because the Ivory Coast is very far from the United States.
Et comment!	I should say so!
Jean et Marie savent parler français mais ils ne connaissent pas aucune personne africaine.	John and Mary know how to speak French but they do not know any African person.
En plus, ils ne connaissent pas le pays.	They are not acquainted with the country either.
Jean va conduire une voiture en Afrique.	John is going to drive a car in Africa.
Ils ont beaucoup de bagages parce qu'ils vont y rester pendant un mois.	They have a lot of luggage because they are going to stay there for a month.
Le numéro de vol est Air France 242 (deux cent quarante-deux) à destination de Paris.	The flight number is Air France 242 to Paris.

A Paris il faut faire escale et puis continuer à Abidjan.

It is necessary to stopover in Paris and then continue to Abidjan.

L'avion (m) décolle de New York à dix heures du matin.

The plane takes off from New York at 10:00 A.M.

Leurs bagages ne pèsent pas trop.

Their luggage does not weigh too much.

La stewardesse et le steward leur servent le déjeuner.

The flight attendants serve them lunch.

Oh, mon Dieu, Jean!

Oh, goodness gracious, John!

J'ai peur et je suis malade.

I'm afraid and I'm sick.

Alors, chérie, pourquoi ne fermes-tu pas les yeux et essayes de dormir un peu?

Well, darling, why don't you close your eyes and try to sleep a little?

Dormir? Si seulement c'était possible!

Sleep? If only I could!

En arrivant à l'aéroport à Abidjan, il leur faut passer la douane.

On arriving at the airport in Abidjan they have to go through customs.

Ils montrent leurs passeports (m) et puis ils répondent à quelques questions.

They show their passports and then they answer several questions.

S'il vous plaît, votre nom

Your name, please

votre nationalité

your nationality

votre situation de famille

your marital status

marié, célibataire, divorcé

married, single, divorced

votre port de sortie

port of exit

votre port d'entrée

port of entry

Ils lui donnent un pourboire.

They give him a tip.

Joseph me donne un livre.

Joseph gives me a book.

Antoine nous montre un plan de la ville.

Anthony shows us a plan of the city.

Je te dis toujours la vérité.

I always tell you the truth.

PLEASE NOTE:
Most of the countries of West Africa have French as their official language. However, the tourist is well advised not to travel in this area today. The extreme poverty has caused discontent and vandalism.

EXPLANATION:

1. There are two ways to translate "to know" into French:

    a. "Connaître" means to know a person, place or thing in the sense of being acquainted with them:

je connais	nous connaissons
tu connais	vous connaissez
il connait	ils connaissent
elle connait	elles connaissent

Nous connaissons nos voisins.	We know our neighbors.
Je connais New York.	I know New York.
Guillaume connait cette cathédrale.	William knows that cathedral.

    b. "Savoir" means to know how to do something or to know a fact or a thing:

        See page 36 for conjugation.

Jean sait conduire.	John knows how to drive.
Je sais que vous prenez des vacances.	I know that you are on vacation.
Elles savent la leçon de français.	They know the French lesson.

2. The French use "en" plus a verb form ending in "ant" to express "upon" doing something:

En arrivant à l'aéroport, j'ai vu mon mari.	Upon arriving at the airport, I saw my husband.
En parlant souvent, nous aprenons le français.	By (upon) speaking often we learn French.
En arrivant a l' aéroport à Abidjan, il leur faut passer la douane.	On arriving at the airport in Abidjan, they must go through customs.

This form, which ends in "ing" in English, is formed in French by dropping the "ons" ending of the "nous" form and substituting "ant."

parler	nous parlons	parlant
choisir	nous choisissons	choisissant
vendre	nous vendons	vendant

3. The words "me" - to me, "te" - to you, "lui" - to him, to her, "nous" - to us, and "leur" - to them are usually placed before the verb:

Ils lui donnent un pourboire.	They give him a tip. (a tip to him)
Je te dis toujours la vérité.	I always tell you the truth. (the truth to you)

CULTURE:

France can be very proud of its transportation system. The trains are run by the government. The fastest train in the world (TGV) travels long distances at 186 miles per hour. Other long-distance trains are "le rapide" and "l'express." There is a local train which stops at every station along the line. Travel is made convenient at the train stations by color schemes and many signs. The stations are crowded but very efficient. Travelers will find the shops, cafés, and restaurants very convenient.

The bus is the most frequent means of local transportation but, in large cities (Paris, Lyons, Lille, and Marseilles) there are subway systems (le métro). Besides city travel these trains will take you to the suburbs. City driving is difficult for most Americans, but, if you plan to go out to the countryside, rent a car.

"Le camping" is very popular among the French people. When traveling, Europeans often stay at camp sites in their colorful tents.

France has co-produced with the British the supersonic transport plane, le Concorde. It is very expensive to fly on the Concorde. If you use Air France to go to France or Africa, your trip will start with your embarcation point: language, food, atmosphere are French.

Means of air and train transportation are centered in Paris so if your plans are to go to a different area of France, you will have to go to Paris to make a connection.

PRACTICE:

1. Prepare a sentence using "savoir" and one using "connaître."

Examples:
Dans cette classe tout le monde sait parler anglais et français. Je n'ai jamais connu ton petit ami.

2. Compose two sentences to ask of your fellow students which require a response of "to me" "to you" etc.

Examples:
A qui est-ce que tu donnes un pourboire? Je lui donne un pourboire. Est-ce que vous nous parlez en espagnol? Non, nous vous parlons en français.

3. Describe a trip to some French-speaking destination. Use your large French vocabulary!

4. In groups of two, prepare a conversation in which one is the questioner and the other answers. Perhaps one is the customs agent, or one might be the tourist and the other the flight attendant. Again, use your imagination.

EXTRA VOCABULARY:
à bord   on board
à vrai dire   to tell the truth
agence de voyage, l' (f)   travel agency
arrivée, l' (f)   arrival
attendre   to wait
billet de première, le   first class ticket
billet de touriste, le   tourist class ticket
C'est à dire.......   That is to say.........
C'est épatant!   It's wonderful!
contre   against
départ, le   departure
durer   to last
ennuyer   to annoy
entre   between
international-e   international
ligne aérienne, la   airline
mettre la ceinture de sécurité   to fasten the seatbelt
monter à bord   to board
moteur, le   motor
Oh, là là   Oh, boy
passager, le   passenger
passagère, la   passenger
pilote, le   pilot

piste, la   runway
rapide   rapid
salle d'attente, la   waiting room
tant mieux   so much the better
valise, la   suitcase
verre gratuit, le   free drink

LESSON 15

LE DIVERTISSEMENT

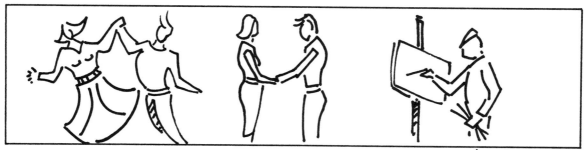

HRVICIN 93

Pierre a invité Linda à sortir
avec lui.
Tu voudrais sortir avec moi,
Linda?
Très volontiers, elle répond.
Où voudrais tu aller?
Bien, commes tu sais, j'aime
beaucoup danser.
Moi, j'aime beaucoup le théatre
et toi, tu aimes danser.
Nous pouvons aller au théatre
d'abord et puis, à un night-club
ou à une discothèque, d'accord?
Oui, mon amour, je m'amuse tou-
jours quand je sors avec toi.

Linda sourit.
Moi, aussi, chéri.
Pierre et Linda s'aiment et ils
ont l'intention de se marier
en juin.
Bien, à sept heures pile.

D'accord, au revoir, Pierre.

Joseph a invité Anne à
passer l'après-midi avec lui.

Peter invited Linda to go out
with him.
Would you like to go out with
me, Linda?
I'd be delighted, she answers.
Where would you like to go?
Well, as you know, I love to
to dance.
I like the theater a lot and you
like to dance.
We can go to the theater first
and then to a club or discotheque,
okay?
Yes, sweetheart, I always have a
good time when I go out with
you.
Linda smiles.
I do, too, honey,
Peter and Linda are in love and
they plan to be married in June.

All right, I'll see you at seven
sharp.
Okay, see you later, Peter.

Joseph invited Anne to spend the
afternoon with him.

Bonjour, Anne, qu'est-ce que vous faites aujourd'hui?

Hello, Anne, what are you doing today?

Je ne suis pas certaine. Puisque je n'ai pas de rendez-vous, je vais regarder la télé.

I'm not sure, Since I don't have a date, I'm going to watch TV.

On peut regarder la télévision n'importe quel jour.

One can watch television any day.

Il fait beau aujourd'hui.

It's a nice day today.

Voulez-vous jouer au tennis ou au golf?

Would you like to play tennis or golf?

Je regrette: je ne joue ni au tennis ni au golf.

I'm sorry: I don't play tennis nor golf.

Voudriez-vous aller à un match de baseball ou de boxe?

Would you like to go to a baseball game or a boxing match?

Je n'aime pas la boxe mais j'aime beaucoup le baseball.

I don't like boxing but I like baseball a lot.

Deux amoureux regardent la télévision.

Two sweethearts are watching television.

Qui a allumé la télé?

Who put the TV on?

Mon petit frère.

My kid brother.

Ton petit frère! Lui, il aime les feuilletons mélos?

Your little brother! Does <u>he</u> like soaps?

Tais-toi! Ce beau blond embrasse sa petite amie. Ils s'embrassent.

Be quiet! That handsome blond is hugging his girlfriend. They're kissing.

A propos, Barbara, où es la bière?

By the way, Barbara, where's the beer?

Comme toujours, dans le réfrigérateur.

As usual, in the refrigerator.

Puis-je changer de programme?

May I change the program?

Je voudrais écouter les actualités.

I would like to listen to the news.

Dans seulement dix minutes.

In just ten minutes.

Est-ce que je peux prendre encore une bière?

May I have another beer?

Mais oui.

Of course.

Plus tard.

Later.

Eh bien, David. Tu es ivre!

Gee, David, you're drunk!

EXPLANATION:

1. Some French comparatives, like their English equivalents, are irregular:

bon, bonne	good	meilleur-e	better
bien	well	mieux	better

Elle est une bonne actrice.	She is a good actress.
Mais Marc est un meilleur acteur.	But Marco is a better actor.
Il chante bien.	He sings well.
Hélène chante mieux.	Helen sings better.

2. In Lesson 12, we studied verbs in which the same person who performs the action receives the action (Je me lave. - I wash myself.). An extension of this idea is "se" meaning "each other" or "to one another."

Suzanne et Jean s'aiment.	Susan and John are in love. (They love each other.)

"Nous" can also mean "each other" or "to one another."

Nous nous écrivons souvent.	We often write to one another.

3. In Lesson 13, Explanation #4, we learned how to form a past tense by using a form of "avoir" and a past participle (J'ai parlé.). Some French verbs require "être" instead of "avoir" for the helping verb. For the most part these verbs indicate "coming" or "going":

arriver	arrivé	arrived
partir	parti	left
entrer	entré	entered
sortir	sorti	gone out
aller	allé	gone
venir	venu	come
rentrer	rentré	returned
rester	resté	stayed

Je suis resté chez moi.	I stayed (have stayed) at home.
Joseph est revenu à Boston.	Joseph returned (has returned) to Boston.

Elles sont entrées dans leur classe.

They entered (have entered) their class.

Nous sommes sortis de bonne heure.

We went (have gone) out early.

Notice that when a past tense verb is conjugated with "être", the past participle, like adjectives, has to be the same gender and number as the person performing the action.

4. "Si" replaces "oui" after a negative question:

Tu n'as pas d'argent? Si, j'en ai beaucoup.
You have no money? Yes, I have a lot (of it).
Pierre n'est pas revenu? Si, il est au salon.
Peter hasn't returned? Yes, he's in the living room.
Tu n'as pas peur de ce chien? Si, j'ai peur du chien!
You're not afraid of this dog? Yes, I'm afraid of the dog!

5.   rire   to laugh

je ris	nous rions
tu ris	vous riez
il rit	ils rient
elle rit	elles rient

Sourire - to smile, is conjugated like rire.

CULTURE:

In France, school is free and compulsory from the age of five to 16 and education is controlled by the State. A student has to work very hard to go on to college. A test is administered at the age of 11 to establish whether the student is "college material." Students who pass the exam, may go to the lycée (high school) and, at the age of 18, after qualifying by passing the baccalauréat exam, on to l'Université. The exams to pass from one school level to the next are extremely difficult in France. The lycée corresponds to our high school and one or two years of college.

It is surprising to American students to learn that French students at the University level are not required to attend class or hand in papers. The truth is that the courses are so difficult that most students do attend classes in order to pass final exams.

Generally speaking, there is a rather formal relationship between student and teacher. The teacher presents the facts, explains and/or interprets them, and the student accepts and learns them.
Some French pastimes are movies, television, newspapers, and card games. American films are very popular in Europe. One often sees people playing checkers and dominoes in the park.

PRACTICE:
1. Invite someone to go someplace with you. Be specific about when and where.

2. Ask questions using the past tense. Your fellow students will have to listen carefully to notice whether you have used "avoir" or "être" so that they will answer correctly.

3. A student starts a story, using two or three sentences. Go around the class, each student adding another two or three sentences, and notice how well you now speak and understand French!

EXTRA VOCABULARY:
activité l' (f)   activity
amuser   to entertain
assister à   to attend
baiser, le   kiss
chanson, la   song
coquin, le   coquine, la   scoundrel
danse, la   dance
équipe, l' (f)   team
être de bonne humeur   to be in a good mood
faire du ski   to ski
film, le   film, movie
fin de semaine, la   week-end
gentil, ille   friendly
gras, se   fat
J'en suis bien content-e.   I'm glad of it.
jaloux, ouse   jealous
mince   slender
nager   to swim
numéro de téléphone, le   telephone number
passe-temps, le   pastime, hobby
piscine, la   swimming pool
plage, la   beach

radio, la   radio
se reposer   to rest
soirée, la   social gathering
sport, le   sport
tendre   affectionate
toujours   forever
vacances, les   vacation
vidéocassette, la   video tape
week-end, le   weekend

This vocabulary includes all of the French words used in the book with the exception of proper nouns, subject pronouns, object pronouns, and numbers. Verbs are presented only in the infinitive form unless they have a special use. Adjectives are presented in the masculine and feminine singular forms. The definite article follows the noun to indicate gender. Abbreviations used are f-feminine, m- masculine.

A

à   to, at
A la semaine prochaine.   See you next week.
à bientôt   see you soon
à bord   on board
à côté de   next to, beside
à demain   see you tomorrow
à destination de   to
à droite   to the right
à gauche   to the left
à la maison   home
à midi   at noon
à pied   on foot
à propos   by the way
à quelle heure   at what time
à vrai dire   to tell the truth
accident, l' (m)   accident
accompagner   accompany
acheter   to buy
acteur, l'   actor
activité, l' (f)   activity
actrice, l'   actress
actualités, les (f)   news
actuel   current
adieu   good-bye
adresse, l' (f)   address
aéroport l' (m)   airport
affaires, les (f)   business

agence de voyage, l' (f)   travel agency
Ah, mon Dieu!   Oh, my goodness!
aider   to help
aller   to go, to be (health)
aller à l'etranger   to go abroad
aller à pied   walk
allergique   allergic
Allô.   Hello (answer to a telephone call).
Allons donc.   Come on now. Really?
Allons-y   Come on, let's go
allumer la télé   put on the TV
alors   then
ami, l' (m)   friend
amie l' (f)   friend
amour, l' (m)   love
amoureux, les (m)   sweethearts
amusant-e   entertaining
amuser   to entertain
amuser, s'   to have a good time
an, l' (m)   year
année, l' (f)   year
annonce, l' (f)   advertisement

août   August
appareil photo, l' (m)
 camera
apparement   apparently
appartement, l' (f)
apartment
appeler, s'   to be called
appendice, l' (m)   appendix
appétit, l' (m)   appetite
apporter   to bring
après   after
après-midi, l' (m)
afternoon
architecte, l' (m)   architect
argent, l' (m)   silver, money
armoire, l' (f)   closet
arrivée, l' (f)   arrival
arriver   to arrive
aspirine l' (f)   aspirin
assez   enough
assiette, l' (f)   dish
assister à   to attend
asseoir, s'   to sit down
assurance, l' (f)   insurance
Attendez un moment!   Just
a minute!
attendre   to wait
Attention!   Watch out!
aucun-e   any
au contraire   on the contrary
au dessus de   on, over
aujourd'hui   today
au lieu de   instead of
au moins   at least
au revoir   so long
Au secours!   Help!
aussi   too, also
autant de   as much as
auteur, l' (m)   author
autobus, l' (m)   bus
automne, l' (m)   autumn
autre   other
avant   before

avec   with
avocat, l' (m)   lawyer
avoir   to have
avoir de la visite   to have
company
avoir l'intention de   to
plan to
avortement, l' (m)
abortion
avril   April

B

bagages, les (m)   luggage
bague, la   ring
baguette, la   long slim loaf
of French bread
baiser, le   kiss
baisser   to lower
balance, la   scales
banlieue, la   outskirts
banque, la   bank
bar, la   bar
bas, les (m)   stockings
beau, belle   pretty,
handsome
beaucoup   very much
beau-fils, le   son-in-law
beau-frère, le   brother-in-
law
beau-père, le   father-in-
law
belle-fille, la   daughter-in-
law
belle-mère, la   mother-in-
law
belle-soeur, la   sister-in-law
beurre, le   butter
bibliothèque, la   library
bien   well
bien sûr   of course
Bienvenu-e!   Welcome!
bière, la   beer

bifteck, le   steak
bijoux, les (m)   jewelry
billet, le   bill, ticket
billet aller et retour, le
round trip ticket
billet de première, le   first
class ticket
billet de touriste, le
tourist class ticket
blanc, che   white
blanchisserie, la   laundry
blessure, la   wound, injury
bleu-e   blue
blond-e   blond
boire   to drink
bois, le   woods
boisson gazeuse, la   soda
boîte, la   can, box
bon, bonne   good
Bon Anniversaire   Happy
Birthday
Bon appetit!   Good appetite
Bon voyage!   Have a good
trip!
bonjour   good day
Bonne Année   Happy New
Year
bonne nuit   good night
bonsoir   good evening
bouche, la   mouth
boucherie, la   butcher shop
boucles d'oreilles, les (f)
earrings
boulangerie, la   bakery
shop
bouteille, la   bottle
boutique, la   shop
bracelet, le   bracelet
bras, le   arm
brochure touristique, la
tourist booklet
brosse à dents, la
toothbrush

bruit, le   noise
brun-e   brown
bureau de poste, le   post
office

C

ça   that
Ça dépend.   It depends.
Ça marche.   Okay, all right.
Ça marche?   How is it
going?
Ça suffit!   That will do!
cadeau, le   gift
cafard, le   cockroach
café, le   café, coffee
café noir, le   black coffee
caisse, la   cashier
caissier, le   caissière, la
bank teller
calculatrice, la   calculator
calorie, la   calorie
carte, la   map, menu
carte postale, la   postcard
cas urgent, le   emergency
casse-croûte, le   snack
causer   to chat
ce, cet, cette, ces   this, that,
these, those
C'est à dire.......   That is to
say.........
C'est ça.   That's right.
C'est dommage.   It's too
bad.
C'est épatant!   It's
wonderful!
C'est pas vrai!   You don't
say!
C'est tout.   That's all.
ceinture, la   waist
Cela dépend.   It depends.
célèbre   famous
célébrer   to celebrate

103

célibataire   single, not married
centre, le   center
certain-e   sure
chaise, la   chair
chambre, la   room
chambre à coucher, la   bedroom
champ, le   field
chance, la   luck
changer   to change
chanson, la   song
chapeau, le   hat
chaque   each, every
charpentier, le   carpenter
chat, le   cat
chatain-e   chestnut colored
chaud-e   hot
chausser   to wear shoes
chaussettes, les (f)   socks
chaussons, les (m)   slippers
chemise, la   shirt
cher, chère   dear, expensive
chercher   to look for
chéri, chérie   dear
cheveux, les (m)   hair
chez   at the home of
chien, le   dog
choisir   to choose
chose, la   thing
ciel, le   the sky
cinéma, le   movies
citron pressé, le   French lemonade
citronnade, la   bottled lemonade
client, le, la   client
climatisation, la   air conditioning
code postal, le   "zip" code
coeur, le   heart

coiffeur, le, coiffeuse, la   hairdresser
coin, le   corner
collants, les (m)   pantyhose
collier, le   necklace
combien   how many
comencer   to begin
comme ci, comme ça   so-so
comment   how
compact disque, le   CD
compagne de chambre, la   roommate
compagnie, la   company
compagnon de chambre, le   roommate
complet, le   suit
comprendre   to understand
comprimé, le   tablet
compris   included
comptoir, le   counter
conduire   to drive
confiture, la   jam
confortable   comfortable
constipation, la   constipation
content-e   happy
continuer   to continue
contre   against
coq au vin, le   chicken in wine sauce
coquin, le   coquine, la   scoundrel
cornflakes, les   cornflakes
corps, le   body
correct-e   correct
costume, le   costume
côte, la   coast
coucher, se   to go to bed
coudre   to sew
couleur, la   color
couple, le   married couple

cousin, le, cousine, la cousin
couteau, le   knife
coûter   to cost
crampes, les (f)   cramps
cravate, la   tie
crayon, le   pencil
crème, la   cream
crème caramel, la   caramel custard
crier   to shout
croissant, le   crescent roll
croque-monsieur, le cheese sandwich with ham
cueillir   to pick
cuillère, la   spoon
cuir, le   leather
cuire   to cook
cuisine, la   kitchen
cuisinier, le   male cook
cuisinière, la   female cook
curé, le   priest

D

dans   in
dans un petit moment   in just a minute
danse, la   dance
danser   to dance
date, la   date
de   of, from
d'abord   at first
d'accord   right, agreed
d'ailleurs   besides
de bonne heure   early
d'ordinaire   ordinarily
de rien   you're welcome
de temps en temps   from time to time
décembre   December
déclarer   to declare
décoller   to take off

défilé, le   parade
dehors   outside
déjeuner, le   lunch
déjeuner   to have lunch
délicieux-se   delicious
demain   tomorrow
demander   to ask for
demeurer   to live
demi-e   half
dentifrice, le   tooth paste
dentiste, le   dentist
dents, les (m)   teeth
départ, le   departure
dépenser   to spend
déposer   to deposit
derrière   behind
derrière, le   buttocks
descendre   to come down, descend
désirer   to want, to desire
dessert, le   dessert
devant   in front of
devenir   to become
devoir   should, ought to
devoir, le   task, homework
diabète, le   diabetes
diarhée, la   diarrhea
Dieu merci!   Thank goodness!
difficile   difficult
dimanche   Sunday
dîner, le   dinner
diplomat, le, diplomate, la diplomat
dire   to say, to tell
directeur, le   manager
discothèque, la discotheque
divertissement, le amusement
doigt, le   finger
dollar, le   dollar

dormir   to sleep
dos, le   the back
douane, la   customs
doux, se   sweet
drap, le   sheet
droit, le   right
durer   to last

E

eau, l' (f)   water
eau minérale, l' (f)   mineral water
échec, l' (m)   failure
école, l' (f)   school
écouter   to listen
écrire   to write
édifice, l' (m)   building
église, l' (f)   church
embrasser   to hug, to kiss
emploi, l' (m)   job
employé-e, l'   employee
emprunt, l' (m)   the loan
emprunter   to borrow
en   in
en arrière   backward, behind
en bonne santé   healthy
en ce moment   right now
en-dessous de   under
en même temps   at the same time
en plein air   outside
encaisser un cheque   to cash a check
enceinte   pregnant
enchanté-e   charmed (used when one is introduced)
encore une fois   again
enfant, l' (m,f)   child
ennuyer   to annoy
enseigner   to teach
ensuite   then, next

entre   between
entrer   to enter
Entrez!   Come in!
enveloppe, l' (f)   envelope
envie, l' (f)   desire, wish
envoyer   to send
épicé-e   spicy
épicerie, l' (f)   grocery store
équipe, l' (f)   team
essayer   to try on
essayer de   to try to
estimer   estimate, gauge
et   and
été, l' (m)   summer
étranger, étrangère, l'   foreigner
être   to be
être de bonne humeur   to be in a good mood
être humain, l' (m)   human being
étudiant, étudiante, l'   student
étudier   to study
excellent-e   excellent
excusez-moi   excuse me
exercice, l' (m)   exercise

F

fâché-e   angry
fâcher, se   to get angry
facile   easy
facteur, le   mailman
facture, la   bill
faible   weak
faim, la   hunger
faire   to make, to do
faire du camping   to camp
faire du ski   to ski
faire escale   to stopover
faire la queue   to stand on line

faire la sieste   to take a nap
faire la valise   to pack one's suitcase
faire le ménage   to do the housework
faire le plein   to fill it up
faire les adieux   to take leave
faire un voyage   to take a trip
faire une demande d'emploi   to apply for a job
faire une promenade   to go for a walk
Faites le plein.   Fill it up.
fatigué-e   tired
fausse couche, la   miscarriage
fauteuil, le   armchair
félicitations   congratulations
femme, la   woman, wife
femme auteur, la   authoress
fenêtre, la   window
fermer   to close
fête, la   party, holiday
feuilleton mélo, le   soap
feux d'artifices, les   (m) fireworks
février   February
fier, fière   proud
fièvre, la   fever
figure, la   face
fille, la   daughter
film, le   film
fils, le   son
fin de semaine, la   week-end
finir   to finish
fou, folle   foolish, mad
fourchette, la   fork
frais, fraîche   fresh, cool
frère, le   brother
froid, le   cold, coldness

fromage, le   cheese
fruits, les (m)   fruit

G

gagner   to earn
gants, les (m)   gloves
garage, le   garage
garçon, le   young boy, guy
gare, la   railroad station
garer   park
gâté-e   spoiled
gâteau, le   cake
genou, le   knee
gens, les (m)   people
gentil, ille   friendly, nice
glace, la   ice, ice cream
goût, le   taste, flavor
goûter   to taste
grand magasin, le   department store
grand-e   big
grand-mère, la   grandmother
grand-père, le   grandfather
grands-parents, les   grandparents
gras, se   fat
gratte-ciel, le   skyscraper greetings
grille-pain, le   toaster
gris-e   gray
grossir   to put on weight

H

habileté, l' (f)   skill, ability
habiter   to live
hamburger, l' (m)   hamburger
haricots, les (m)   beans
haut-e   high, tall
heure, l' (f)   hour

heureux-se   happy
hier   yesterday
hiver, l' (m)   winter
homme, l'   man
homme d'affaires, l'
business man
honte, la   shame
hôpital, l' (m)   hospital
hors d'oeuvres, les (m)
appetizers
hôstesse. l'   stewardess
hot dog, le   hot dog
huile, l' (f)   oil

I

il faut   it is necessary
il y a   there is, there are
imperméable, l' (m)
raincoat
infirmier, l' , infirmière, l'
nurse
ingénieur, l' (m)   engineer
injection, l' (f)   injection
insolation, l' (f)   sunstroke
insomnie, l' (f)   insomnia
intelligent-e   intelligent
intéréssant-e   interesting
intérêt, l' (m)   interest
international-e
international
intolérable   really bad
inviter   to invite
iode, l' (m)   iodine
ivre   drunk

J

J'en suis bien content-e.
I'm glad of it.
jaloux, ouse   jealous
jamais   never
jambe, la   leg

jambon, le   ham
janvier   January
jaquette, la   jacket
jardin, le   garden
jaune   yellow
Je crois que oui.   I believe so.
Je suis désolé.   I am so
sorry.
jeudi   Thursday
jeune fille, la   young girl
jeune   young
joli-e   pretty
jouer   to play
jouer au golf   to play golf
jouer au tennis   to play
tennis
jouer aux cartes   to play
cards
jouer du piano   to play the
piano
jouet, le   toy
jour, le   day
jour ouvrable, le   work day
Joyeux Noël   Merry
Christmas
juillet   July
juin   June
jupe, la   skirt
jus d'orange, le   orange
juice
jusque   up to, until

L

là   there
là-bas   over there
L'addition, (f) s'il vous
plaît.   The bill, please.
laid-e   ugly
lait, le   milk
lard, le   bacon
large   wide
laver, se   to wash up

laxatif, le   laxative
légume, le   vegetable
lentement   slowly
lettre, la   letter
lever, se   to stand up
ligne aérienne, la   airline
lire   to read
lit, le   bed
livre, la   pound
livre, le   book
loin   far
long, ue   long
louer   to rent
lourd-e   heavy
lundi   Monday
lunettes, les (f)   glasses
luxeux-se   luxurious

M

machine à laver, la
washing machine
madame   ma'am, Mrs.
mademoiselle   Miss
Magnifique!   Great!
mai   May
maigrir   to slim down
maillot de bain, le   bathing
suit
main, la   hand
mais   but
mal   badly
malade   sick
maladie, la   illness, sickness
malheureusement
unfortunately
mandat-postal, le   money
order
manger   to eat
manteau, le   coat
maquillage, le   make-up
marchander   to bargain
marché-e   inexpensive

marcher   to walk
mardi   Tuesday
mari, le   husband
mariage, le   wedding
marier, se   to get married
mars   March
masque, le   mask
match de baseball, le
baseball game
match de boxe, le   boxing
match
matin, le   the morning, in
the morning
mauvais-e   bad
mécanicien, le   mechanic
médecin, le   doctor
médicament, le   medicine
(medication)
médicine, la   medical
profession
meilleur-e   better
ménagère, la   homemaker
mentir   to lie
merci   thank you
mercredi   Wednesday
mère, la   mother
mériter   to deserve
merveilleux, merveilleuse
marvelous
mes amitiés à Marie
Greetings or regards to Mary
métier, le   occupation
métro, le   subway
mettre   to put
mettre de coté   to save
(money)
mettre la ceinture de
sécurité   to fasten the
seatbelt
mettre la lettre à la poste
to mail the letter
meubles, les (m)   furniture
midi, le   noon

mince   slender
minuit, le   midnight
miroir, le   mirror
moderne   modern
Moi non plus.   Nor I.
moins   less
mois, le   month
monsieur   Sir, Mr.
montant, le   amount
monter à bord   to board
montre-bracelet, la   wrist watch
montrer   to show
moteur, le   motor
mouchoir, le   handkerchief
mouillé-e   wet

N

nager   to swim
nationalité, la   nationality
nécessaire   necessary
neige, la   snow
neiger   to snow
net, te   clean
nettoyer   to clean
neveu, le   nephew
nez, le   nose
ni   nor, neither
nièce, la   niece
night-club, le   club
noir-e   black
noix, la   nut
nom, le   name
non   no
non plus   either
nourriture, la   food
nouveau, nouvelle   new
novembre   November
numéro, le   number
numéro de téléphone, le telephone number

O

objet, l' (m)   article
occupé-e   busy
octobre   October
oeuf, l' (m)   egg
Oh, c'est affreux!   Oh, it's awful!
Oh, là là   Oh, boy
oignon, l' (m)   onion
oiseau, l' (m)   bird
omelette, l' (f)   omelet
on doit   one should, ought to
oncle, l'   uncle
ongles, les (m)   fingernails
or, l' (m)   gold
orange, l' (f)   orange
orangé-e   orange
orchestre, l' (m)   orchestra
ordonnance, l' (f) prescription
oreiller, l' (m)   pillow
ou   or
où   where
oublier   to forget
Ouf!   Phew!
oui   yes
ouvrir un compte   to open an account

P

pain, le   bread
pain grillé, le   toast
palais, le   palace
pantalon, le   pants
papier, le   paper
papier hygiénique, le toilet tissue
paquet, le   package
par avion   airmail
par exemple   for example

par ici around here, this way

parapluie, la umbrella

pardon pardon me

parents, les parents, relatives

parfumerie, la perfume shop

parler to speak

partir depart

pas du tout not at all

passager, le, passagère, la passenger

passeport, le passport

passe-temps, le pastime, hobby

passer to spend, to pass

patron, le boss

pauvre poor

payer to pay

pays, le country

paysage, le landscape

peigner, se to comb one's hair

pendant during

penser to think

perdre to lose

père, le father

permis de conduire, le driver's license

Perrier cassis, le blackcurrent soft drink

personne no one

personne, la person

peser to weigh

petit-e little, small

petit déjeuner, le breakfast

petit-fils, le grandson

petite cuillère, la teaspoon

petite-fille, la grandaughter

petits pains, les (m) rolls

petits-pois, les (m) peas

peu à peu little by little

peur, la fear

peut-être perhaps

pharmacie, la drug store

pièce, la coin, room

pieds, les (m) feet

pile sharp, on the dot

piscine, la swimming pool

piste, la runway

place, la seat

plage, la beach

plat, le dish

plat international, le foreign dish

plein-e full

pleuvoir to rain

plonger to dive

pluie, la rain

plus more

plus ou moins more or less

plus que jamais more than ever

plus tard later

plusieurs several

poche, la pocket

poisson, le fish

poitrine, la chest

poivre, le pepper

poli-e polite

pomme, la apple

pomme de terre, la potato

pommes frites, les (f) fried potatoes, French fries

porc, le pork

port d'entrée, le port of entry

port de sortie, le port of exit

portefeuille, le wallet

porter to take, to carry, to wear

porteur, le porter

poulet, le chicken
poupée, la doll
pour for
pourboire, le tip
pourcentage, le percentage
pourpre purple
pourquoi why
pouvoir can, to be able
préférer to prefer
premier, ière first
prendre to take
prendre une photo to take
a snapshot
présenter introduce,
present
préservatif, le condom
presque almost
prêter to lend
printemps, le spring
prix, le price, prize
problème, le problem
professeur, le professor,
teacher (m,f)
profession, la profession
programmeur, le
programmeuse, la
computer programmer
prononcer to pronounce
propriétaire, le owner
provisions, les (f) groceries
psychologue, le, la
psychologist
puis then
pullover, le sweater
pyjama, le pajamas

Q

qualité, la quality
quand when
quart, le quarter
Quel dommage! What a
shame! What a pity!

quelque chose something
quelquefois sometimes
quelqu'un someone
question, la question
Qui sait? Who knows?
quoi what
Quoi de neuf? What's new?

R

radio, la radio
raisin, le grape
raison, la reason, right
rapide rapid
raser to shave
ravi-e delighted
récemment recently,
freshly
recevoir receive
réfrigérateur, le
refrigerator
regarder to look, to look at
régime, le diet
remplir to fill out (a form)
rendez-vous, le date,
meeting
rendre to return (give back)
renvoyer to fire
répéter to repeat
répondre to answer
reposer, se to rest
réserver to reserve
respirer to breathe
restaurant, le restaurant
rester to remain, to stay
retirer to withdraw
retourner to return
réussir to succeed
revenir to return
revenu, le income
revue, la magazine
rhum, le rum

rhume, le   cold
riche   rich
rien   nothing
rire   to laugh
risque, le   risk
riz, le   rice
robe, la   dress
rose   pink
rouge   red
rougir   to blush
route, la   highway
rue, la   street

S

s'il vous plaît   please
sac à main, le   handbag
saison, la   season
salade, la   salad
salaire, le   salary
sale   dirty
salle à manger, la   dining room
salle d'attente, la   waiting room
salle de bain, la   bathroom
salon, le   beauty shop, living room
saluer   to greet
salut   hello, goodbye,
samedi   Saturday
sandwich, le   sandwich
sans doute   no doubt, doubtless
santé, la   health
Santé!   To your health!
saucisse, la   sausage
sauver (la vie)   to save (a life)
savoir   to know
savon, le   soap
sec, sèche   dry
secrétaire, le, la   secretary

sein, le   bosom
sel, le   salt
selon   according to
semaine, la   week
septembre   September
serveur, le   waiter
service, le   service charge
serviette hygiènique, la   sanitary napkin
serviette, la   towel, briefcase
servir   to serve, wait on
seulement   only
shampooing, le   shampoo
SIDA, le   AIDS
sieste, la   nap
simpathique   pleasant
situation de famille, la   marital status
soeur, la   sister
sofa, la   sofa
soif, la   thirst
soir, le   evening
soirée, la   social gathering
soirée dansante, la   dance
soldat, le   soldier
soleil, le   sun
sommeil, le   sleepiness
sommelier, le   wine steward
sortir   to go out
soulier, les (m)   shoes
sourire   to smile
souris, la   mouse
sous-sol, le   basement
sous-vêtements, les (m)   underwear
soutien-gorge, le   bra
souvent   often
sparadrap, le   adhesive tape
steward, le   stewardesse, la   flight attendants
stylo, le   pen
sucre, le   sugar
suivant-e   following

supermarché, le supermarket

surpris-e surprised

symptôme, le symptom

T

table, la table

tableau, le picture

taire, se to be quiet

tampon, le tampon

tant mieux so much the better

tante, la aunt

tapis, le carpet

tard late

tarifs postaux, les (m) postage

tasse, la cup

taux de change, le rate of exchange

taxi, le taxi

teindre to tint

télé, la TV

téléphone, le telephone

téléphoner to telephone

télévision, la television

témoin, le witness

tempête, la storm

temps, le weather

tendre affectionate

tête, la head

thé, le tea

théatre, le theater

thermomètre, le thermometer

timbre, le stamp

toilettes, les (f) toilets

tonnerre, le thunder

tôt soon

toucher le chèque to cash the check

toujours forever

tous les jours every day

tout everything

tout à l'heure soon

tout de suite right away

tout droit straight ahead

tout le monde everybody

toux, la cough

traduire translate

train, le train

travail, le work

travailler to work

très very

Très bonne idée. That's a fine idea.

triste sad

trop too much

troupe, la group

trouver, se to be located

tutoyer to use the informal "you"

typique typical

U

un peu a little

université, l' (f) university

utile useful

V

vacances, les (f) vacation

valise, la suitcase

valoir to be worth

vendeur, le shop assistant

vendre to sell

vendredi Friday

venir to come

vent, le wind

vente, la sale

ventre, le stomach

vérité, la truth

verre, le glass

verre de champagne, le
glass of champagne

verre gratuit, le   free drink

vers   toward

vert-e   green

vêtements, les (m)
clothing

veuf, le   widower

veuve, la   widow

viande, la   meat

vieux, vieille   old

village, le   town

ville, la   city

vin, le   wine

vin blanc, le   white wine

vin rouge, le   red wine

visa, le   visa

visage, le   face

visiter   to visit

vite   quickly

voie, la   track

voir   to see

voiture, la   car

vol, le   flight, theft

voler   to fly, to steal

volontiers   gladly

vomissement, le   vomiting

voter   to vote

vouloir   to want

vousvoyer   to use the
formal "you"

voyage d'affaires, le
business trip

voyage de noce, le
honeymoon

voyager   to travel

Voyons!   Let's see! Come on!

vraiment   really

W

week-end, le   weekend

whisky, le   whiskey

Y

y a-t-il   is there, are there

yeux, les (m)   eyes

A

a little   un peu
ability   l'habileté (f)
abortion   l'avortement (m)
accident   l'accident (m)
accompany   accompagner
according to   selon
activity   l'activité (f)
actor   l'acteur
actress   l'actrice
address   l'adresse (f)
adhesive tape   le sparadrap
advertisement   l'anonce (f)
affectionate   tendre
after   après
afternoon   l'après-midi (m)
again   encore une fois
against   contre
agreed   d'accord
AIDS   le SIDA
air conditioning   la climatisation
airline   la ligne aérienne
airmail   par avion
airport   l'aéroport (m)
All right   Ça marche.
allergic   allergique
almost   presque
also   aussi
amount   le montant
amusement   le divertissement
and   et
angry   faché-e
annoy   ennuyer
answer   répondre
any   aucun-e
apparently   apparement

appartment   l'appartement (f)
appendix   l'appendice (m)
appetite   l'appétit (m)
appetizers   les hors d'oeuvres (m)
apple   la pomme
apply for a job   faire une demande d'emploi
April   avril
architect   l'architecte (m)
are there   y a-t-il
arm   le bras
armchair   le fauteuil
around here   par ici
arrival   l'arrivée (f)
arrive   arriver
article   l'objet (m)
as much as   autant de
ask for   demander
aspirin   l'aspirine,(f)
at   à
at first   d'abord
at least   au moins
at noon   à midi
at the home of   chez
at the same time   en même temps
attend   assister à
At what time?   A quelle heure?
August   août
aunt   la tante
author   l'auteur (m)
authoress   femme auteur (la)
autumn   l'automne (m)

B

back   le dos
backward   en arrière
bacon   le lard
bad   mauvais-e
badly   mal
bakery shop   la boulangerie
banana   la banane
bank   la banque
bank teller   le caissier, la caissière
bar   la bar
bargain   marchander
baseball game   le match de baseball
basement   le sous-sol
bathing suit   le maillot de bain
bathroom   la salle de bain
be   être
be able   pouvoir
be called   s'appeler
be in a good mood   être de bonne humeur
be located   se trouver
be quiet   se taire
be worth   valoir
beach   la plage
beans   les haricots (m)
beauty shop   le salon
become   devenir
bed   le lit
bedroom   la chambre à coucher
beer   la bière
before   avant
begin   commencer
behind   derrière, en arrière
beside   à côté de
besides   d'ailleurs
better   meilleur-e
between   entre

big   grand-e
bill (money)   le billet
bill   la facture
bird   l'oiseau (m)
black coffee   le café noir
black current soft drink   Perrier cassis
black   noir-e
blond   blond-e
blue   bleu-e
blush   rougir
board   monter à bord
body   le corps
book   le livre
borrow   emprunter
bosom   le sein
boss   le patron
bottle   la bouteille
box   la boîte
boxing match   le match de boxe
boy   le garçon
bra   le soutien-gorge
bracelet   le bracelet
bread (long slim loaf)   la baguette
bread   le pain
breakfast   le petit déjeuner
breathe   respirer
briefcase   la serviette
bring   apporter
brother   le frère
brother-in-law   le beau-frère
brown   brun-e
building   l'édifice (m)
bus   l'autobus (m)
business   les affaires (f)
business man   l'homme d'affaires
business trip   le voyage d'affaires
busy   occupé-e

but   mais
butcher shop   la boucherie
butter   le beurre
buttocks   le derrière
buy   acheter
by the way   à propos

C

cake   le gâteau
calculator   la calculatrice
calorie   la calorie
camera   l'appareil (m) photo
camp   faire du camping
can   la boîte
can   pouvoir
car   la voiture
caramel custard   la crème caramel
carpenter   le charpentier
carpet   le tapis
carry   porter
cash a check   encaisser un cheque
cashier   la caisse
cat   le chat
CD   le compact disque
celebrate   célébrer
center   le centre
cescent roll   le croissant
chair   la chaise
change   changer
charmed (used when one is introduced)   enchanté-e
chat   causer
check   le chèque
cheese   le fromage
cheese sandwich with ham   le croque-monsieur
chest   la poitrine
chestnut colored   chatain-e
chicken in wine sauce   le coq au vin

chicken   le poulet
child   l'enfant (m,f)
choose   choisir
church   l'église (f)
city   la ville
clean   net-te
clean   nettoyer
client   le, la cliente
close   fermer
closet   l'armoire (f)
clothing   les vêtements (m)
club   le night-club
coast   la côte
coat   le manteau
cockroach   le cafard
coffee   le café
coin   la pièce
cold (sickness)   le rhume
coldness   le froid
color   la couleur
comb one's hair   se peigner
Come in!   Entrez!
Come on!   Voyons!
Come on now.   Allons donc.
come down   descendre
come   venir
comfortable   confortable
company   la compagnie
computer programmer   le programmeur, la programmeuse
condom   le préservatif
congratulations   félicitations
constipation   la constipation
continue   continuer
cook   cuire
cook   le cuisinier, la cuisinière
cool   frais, fraîche
corner   le coin
cornflakes   les cornflakes
correct   correct-e

cost   coûter
costume   le costume
cough   la toux
counter   le comptoir
country   le pays
couple (married)   le couple
cousin   le cousin, la cousine
cramps   les crampes (f)
cream   la crème
cup   la tasse
current   actuel
customs   la douane

D

dance   danser
dance   la danse
dance   la soirée dansante
date (calendar)   la date
date (meeting)   le rendez-vous
daughter   la fille
daughter-in-law   la belle-fille
day   le jour
dear   cher, chère
dear (sweetheart)   chéri, chérie
December   décembre
delicious   délicieux-se
delighted   ravi-e
dentist   le dentiste
depart   partir
department store   le grand magasin
departure   le départ
deposit   déposer
deserve   mériter
desire   désirer
desire   l'envie (f)
dessert   le dessert
diabetes   le diabète
diarrhea   la diarrhée

diet   le régime
difficult   difficile
dining room   la salle à manger
dinner   le dîner
diplomat   le diplomate, la diplomate
dirty   sale
discotheque   la discothèque
dish   l'assiette (f)
dish (food)   le plat
dive   plonger
do   faire
do the housework   faire le ménage
doctor   le médecin
dog   le chien
doll   la poupée
dollar   le dollar
doubtless   sans doute
dress   la robe
drink   boire
drive   conduire
driver's license   le permis de conduire
drug store   la pharmacie
drunk   ivre
dry   sec, sèche
during   pendant

E

each   chaque
early   de bonne heure
earn   gagner
earrings   les boucles (f) d'oreilles
easy   facile
eat   manger
egg   l'oeuf (m)
either   non plus
emergency   le cas urgent
employee   l'employé-e

120

engineer   l'ingénieur (m)
enough   assez
enter   entrer
entertain   amuser
entertaining   amusant-e
envelope   l'enveloppe (f)
estimate   estimer
evening   le soir
every   chaque
every day   tous les jours
everybody   tout le monde
everything   tout
excerise   l'excercice (m)
excuse me   excusez-moi
expensive   cher, chère
eyes   les yeux (m)

F

face   le visage
failure   l'échec (m)
famous   célèbre
far   loin
fasten the seatbelt   mettre
la ceinture de sécurité
fat   gras-se
father   le père
father-in-law   le beau-père
fear   la peur
February   février
feet   les pieds (m)
fever   la fièvre
field   le champ
fill it up (with gasoline)
faire le plein
fill out (a form)   remplir
film   le film
finger   le doigt
fingernails   les ongles (m)
finish   finir
fire (from a job)   renvoyer
fireworks   les feux d'artifice

first class ticket   le billet
de première
first   premier, première
fish   le poisson
flavor   le goût
flight   le vol
flight attendant   le steward,
la stewardesse
fly   voler
following   suivant-e
food   la nourriture
foolish   fou, folle
for   pour
for example   par exemple
foreign dish   le plat
internatinal
foreigner   l'étranger, l'
étrangère
forever   toujours
forget   oublier
fork   la fourchette
free drink   le verre gratuit
French fries   les pommes
frites (f)
fresh   frais, fraîche
freshly   récemment
Friday   vendredi
fried potatoes   les pommes
frites (f)
friend   l'ami, l'amie
friendly   gentil, ille
from   de
from time to time   de
temps en temps
fruit   les fruits (m)
full   plein-e
furniture   les meubles (m)

G

garage   le garage
garden   le jardin
gauge   estimer

get angry   se fâcher
get married   se marier
get up   se lever
gift   le cadeau
girl   la jeune fille
gladly   volontiers
glass   le verre
glass of champagne   le verre de champagne
glasses   les lunettes (f)
gloves   les gants (m)
go   aller
go abroad   aller à l'étranger
go for a walk   faire une promenade
go out   sortir
go shopping   faire les courses
go to bed   se coucher
gold   l'or (m)
good   bon, bonne
Good appetite!   Bon appetit!
good day   bonjour
good evening   bonsoir
good night   bonne nuit
good-bye   adieu
grandaughter   la petite-fille
grandfather   le grand-père
grandmother   la grand-mère
grandparents   les grands-parents
grandson   le petit-fils
grape   le raisin
gray   gris-e
Great!   Magnifique!
green   vert-e
greet   saluer
greetings   salutations
groceries   les provisions (f)
grocery store   l'épicerie (f)
group   le troupe
guy   le garçon

H

hair   les cheveux (m)
hairdresser   le coiffeur, la coiffeuse
half   demi-e
ham   le jambon
hamburger   le hamburger
hand   la main
handbag   le sac à main
handkerchief   le mouchoir
handsome, pretty   beau
Happy Birthday   Bon Anniversaire
Happy New Year   Bonne Année
happy   content-e, heureux-se
hat   le chapeau
have   avoir
Have a good trip!   Bon voyage!
have a good time   s'amuser
have company   avoir de la visite
have lunch   déjeuner
head   la tête
health   la santé
healthy   en bonne santé
heart   le coeur
heavy   lourd-e
Hello (on telephone)   Allô
help   aider
Help!   Au secours!
high   haut-e
highway   la route
hobby   le passe-temps
holiday   la fête
homemaker   la ménagère
homework   le devoir
honeymoon   le voyage de noce
hospital   l'hôpital (m)

hot   chaud-e
hot dog   le hot dog
hour   l'heure (f)
how   comment
How is it going?   Ça marche?
how many   combien
hug   embrasser
human being   l'être humain (m)
hunger   la faim
husband   le mari

I

I am so sorry.   Je suis désolé-e.
I believe not.   Je crois que non.
I believe so.   Je crois que oui.
I'm glad of it.   J'en suis bien content-e.
ice cream   la glace
ice   la glace
in   dans, en
in front of   devant
in just a minute   dans un petit moment
in the morning   le matin
included   compris
income   le revenu
inexpensive   bon marché
injection   l'injection (f)
injury   la blessure
insomnia   l'insomnie (f)
instead of   au lieu de
insurance   l'assurance (f)
intelligent   intelligent-e
interest   l'intérêt (m)
interesting   interessant-e
international   international-e
introduce   présenter
invite   inviter

iodine   l'iode (m)
is there   y a-t-il
It depends.   Ça dépend.
it is necessary   il faut
It's too bad.   C'est dommage.
It's wonderful!   C'est épatant!

J

jacket   la jaquette
jam   la confiture
January   janvier
jealous   jaloux-se
jewelry   les bijoux (m)
job   l'emploi (m)
July   juillet
June   juin
Just a minute!   Attendez un moment!

K

kiss   embrasser
kiss   le baiser
kitchen   la cuisine
knee   le genou
knife   le couteau
know   savoir

L

landscape   le paysage
large   grand-e
last   durer
late   tard
later   plus tard
laugh   rire
laundry   la blanchisserie
lawyer   l'avocat (m)
laxative   le laxatif
leather   le cuir

leg   la jambe
lemonade   le citron pressé (French style)
lemonade, bottled   la citronnade
lend   prêter
less   moins
Let's go, come on.   Allons-y.
Let's see!   Voyons!
letter   la lettre
library   la bibliothèque
lie   mentir
like   aimer
listen   écouter
little   petit-e
little by little   peu à peu
live   demeurer, habiter
living room   le salon
loan   l'emprunt (m)
long   long-ue
look (at)   regarder
look for   chercher
lose   perdre
love   aimer
love   l'amour
lower   baisser
luck   la chance
luggage   les bagages (m)
lunch   le déjeuner

M

ma'am   madame
mad   fou, folle
magazine   la revue
mail the letter   mettre la lettre à la poste
mailman   le facteur
make   faire
make-up   le maquillage
man   l'homme
manager   le directeur
map   la carte

March   mars
marital status   la situation de famille
marvelous   merveilleux- se
mask   le masque
May   mai
meat   la viande
mechanic   le mécanicien
medical profession   la médicine
medicine (medication)   les médicaments
meeting   le rendez-vous
menu   la carte
Merry Christmas   Joyeux Noël
midnight   le minuit
milk   le lait
mineral water   l'eau minéral (f)
mirror   le miroir
miscarriage   la fausse couche
Miss   mademoiselle
modern   moderne
Monday   lundi
money   l'argent (m)
money order   le mandat-postal
month   le mois
more   plus
more or less   plus ou moins
more than ever   plus que jamais
morning   le matin
mother   la mère
mother-in-law   la belle-mère
motor   le moteur
mouth   la bouche
movies   le cinéma
Mr.   Monsieur
Mrs.   Madame

much beaucoup

N

name le nom
nap la sieste
nationality la nationalité
necklace le collier
neither ni
nephew le neveu
never jamais
new nouveau, nouvelle
news les actualités (f)
next ensuite
next to à côté de
nice gentil, ille
niece la nièce
no non
no one personne
noise le bruit
noon le midi
nor ni
Nor I. Moi non plus.
nose le nez
not at all pas du tout
nothing rien
November novembre
number le numéro
nurse l'infirmier, l'infirmière
nut la noix

O

occupation le métier
October octobre
of de
of course bien sûr
often souvent
Oh, boy. Oh, là, là.
Oh, it's awful! Oh, c'est affreux!

Oh, my goodness! Ah, mon Dieu!
oil l'huile (f)
Okay Ça marche.
old vieux, vielle
omelet l'omelette (f)
on sur
on board à bord
on foot à pied
on the contrary au contraire
on the dot pile
one ought to, one should on doit
onion l'oignon (m)
only seulement
open an account ouvrir un compte
orange juice le jus d'orange
orange l'orange (f)
orange orangé-e
orchestra l'orchestre (m)
ordinarily d'ordinaire
other autre
ought to devoir
outside dehors, en plein air
outskirts la banlieue
over au dessus de
over there là-bas
owner le propriétaire

P

pack one's suitcase faire la valise
package le paquet
pajamas le pyjama
palace le palais
pants le pantalon
pantyhose les collants (m)
paper le papier
parade le défilé
pardon me pardon

parents   les parents
park   garer
party   la fête
pass   passer
passenger   le passager, la passagère
passport   le passeport
pastime   le passe-temps
pay   payer
peas   les petits-pois (m)
pen   le stylo
pencil   le crayon
people   les gens (m)
pepper   le poivre
percentage   le pourcentage
perfume shop   la parfumerie
perhaps   peut-être
person   la personne (m,f)
Phew!   Ouf!
pick   cueillir
picture   le tableau
pillow   l'oreiller (m)
pink   rose
plan to   avoir l'intention de
play   jouer
play cards   jouer aux cartes
play golf   jouer au golf
play tennis   jouer au tennis
play the piano   jouer du piano
pleasant   simpathique
please   s'il vous plaît
pocket   la poche
polite   poli-e
poor   pauvre
pork   le porc
port of entry   le port d'entrée
port of exit   le port de sortie
porter   le porteur

post office   le bureau de poste
postage   les tarifs posteaux (m)
postcard   la carte postale
potato   la pomme de terre
pound   la livre
prefer   préférer
pregnant   enceinte
prescription   l'ordonnance (f)
present   présenter
pretty   beau, belle, joli-e
price   le prix
priest   le curé
prize   le prix
problem   le problème
profession   la profession
professor   le professeur (m,f)
pronounce   prononcer
proud   fier, fière
psychologist   le/la psychologue
purple   pourpre
put   mettre
put on the TV   allumer la télé
put on weight   grossir

Q

quality   la qualité
quarter   le quart
question   la question
quickly   vite

R

radio   la radio
railroad station   la gare
rain   la pluie
rain   pleuvoir
raincoat   l'imperméable (m)
rapid   rapide

rate of exchange   le taux de change
read   lire
really   vraiment
reason   la raison
receive   recevoir
recently   récemment
red   rouge
red wine   le vin rouge
refrigerator   le réfrigérateur
Regards to Mary.   Mes amitiés à Marie.
relatives   les parents
remain   rester
rent   louer
repeat   répéter
reserve   réserver
rest   se reposer
restaurant   le restaurant
return (come back)   revenir
return (give back)   rendre
return   retourner
rice   le riz
rich   riche
right away   tout de suite
right (agreed)   d'accord
right   la raison
right (direction)   le droit
right now   en ce moment
ring   la bague
risk   le risque
rob   voler
rolls   les petits pains (m)
room   la chambre, la pièce
roommate   le compagnon, la compagne de chambre
round trip ticket   le billet aller et retour
rum   le rhum
runway   la piste

S

sad   triste
salad   la salade
salary   le salaire
sale   la vente
salt   le sel
sandwich   le sandwich
sanitary napkin   la serviette hygiénique
Saturday   samedi
sausage   la saucisse
save (a life)   sauver (la vie)
save (money)   mettre de coté
say   dire
scales   la balance
school   l'école (f)
scoundrel   le coquin, la coquine
season   la saison
seat   la place
secretary   le/la secrétaire
see   voir
see you next week.   à la semaine prochaine.
see you soon   à bientôt
see you tomorrow   à demain
sell   vendre
send   envoyer
September   septembre
serve   servir
service charge   le service
several   plusieurs
sew   coudre
shame   l'honte
shampoo   le shampooing
shave   raser
sheet   le drap
shirt   la chemise
shoes   les souliers (m)
shop assistant   le vendeur

shop　la boutique
shout　crier
show　montrer
sick　malade
sign　signer
silver　l'argent (m)
single (unmarried)
célibataire
Sir　Monsieur
sister　la soeur
sister-in-law　la belle soeur
sit down　s'asseoir
ski　faire du ski
skill　l'habileté (f)
skirt　la jupe
sky　le ciel
skyscraper　le gratte-ciel
sleep　dormir
sleepiness　le sommeil
slim down　maigrir
slippers　les chaussons (m)
slowly　lentement
small　petit-e
smile　sourire
snack　le casse-croûte
snow　la neige
snow　neiger
so long　au revoir
so much the better　tant
mieux
so-so　comme ci, comme ça
soap (on TV)　le feuilleton
mélo
soap　le savon
social gathering　la soirée
socks　les chaussettes (f)
soda　la boisson gazeuse
sofa　le sofa
soldier　le soldat
someone　quelqu'un
sometimes　quelquefois
son　le fils
son-in-law　le beau-fils

song　la chanson
soon　tôt, tout à l'heure
speak　parler
spend (money)　dépenser
spend (time)　passer
spicy　épicé-e
spoiled　gâté-e
spoon　la cuillère
spring　le printemps
stamp　le timbre
stand on line　faire la
queue
stay　rester
steak　le bifteck
steal　voler
stockings　les bas (m)
stomach　le ventre
stopover　faire escale
storm　la tempête
straight ahead　tout droit
street　la rue
student　l'étudiant-e
study　étudier
subway　le métro
succeed　réussir
sugar　le sucre
suit　le complet
suitcase　la valise
summer　l'été (m)
sun　le soleil
Sunday　dimanche
sunstroke　l'insolation (f)
supermarket　le
supermarché
sure　certain-e
surprised　surpris-e
sweater　le pullover
sweet　doux-se
sweethearts　les amoureux
swim　nager
swimming pool　la piscine
symtom　le symptôme

T

table   la table
tablet   le comprimé
take (carry)   porter
take (pick up)   prendre
take a nap   faire la sieste
take a snapshot   prendre une photo
take a trip   faire un voyage
take leave   faire les adieux
take off   décoller
tall   haut-e
tampon   le tampon
task   le devoir
taste   goûter
taste   le goût
taxi   le taxi
tea   le thé
teach   enseigner
teacher   le professeur (m,f)
team   l'équipe (f)
teaspoon   la petite cuillère
teeth   les dents (m)
telephone   le téléphone, l'appareil (m)
telephone number   le numéro de téléphone
téléphoner   telephone
television   la télévision
tell   dire
Thank Heavens!   Dieu merci!
thank you   merci
that   ça
That is to say........   C'est à dire............
That will do!   Ça suffit!
That's a fine idea!   Très bonne idée!
That's all.   C'est tout.
That's right.   C'est ça.
The bill, please.   L'addition, s'il vous plaît.

theater   le théatre
theft   le vol
then   alors, puis, ensuite
there   là
there is, there are   il y a
thermometer   le thermometer
thin   mince
thing   la chose
think   penser
thirst   la soif
this way   par ici
this, that   ce, cet, cette, ces
thunder   le tonerre
Thursday   jeudi
ticket   le billet
tie   la cravate
tint   teindre
tip   le pourboire
tired   fatigué-e
to   à
To your health!   Santé!
to tell the truth   à vrai dire
to the left   à gauche
to the right   à droite
to wear shoes   chausser
toast   le pain-grillé
toaster   le grille-pain
today   aujourd'hui
toilet paper   le papier hygiénique
toilets   les toilettes (f)
tomorrow   demain
too   aussi
too much   trop
tooth paste   le dentifrice
toothbrush   la brosse à dents
tourist booklet   la brochure touristique
tourist class ticket   le billet de touriste

toward   vers
towel   la serviette
toy   le jouet
track   la voie
train   le train
translate   traduire
travel   voyager
travel agency   l'agence de voyage (f)
traveler's check   le chèque de voyage
truth   la vérité
try on   essayer
try to   essayer de
Tuesday   mardi
TV   la télé
typical   typique

U

ugly   laid-e
umbrella   la parapluie
unbearable   intolérable
uncle   l'oncle
under   en-dessous de
understand   comprendre
underwear   les sous-vêtements (m)
unfortunately   malheureusement
university   l'université (f)
until   jusque
use the familiar form of "you"   tutoyer
use the formal form of "you"   vousvoyer
useful   utile

V

vacation   les vacances (f)
vegetable   le légume
very   très

village   le village
visit   visiter
vomiting   le vomissement
vote   voter

W

waist   la ceinture
wait   attendre
wait on   servir
waiter   le serveur
waiting room   la salle d'attente
walk   aller à pied, marcher
wallet   le portefeuille
want   désirer, vouloir
wash up   se laver
washing machine   la machine à laver
Watch out!   Attention!
water   l'eau (f)
weak   faible
wear   porter
weather   le temps
wedding   le mariage
Wednesday   mercredi
week   la semaine
week-end   la fin de semaine, le week-end
weigh   peser
Welcome!   Bienvenu-e!
well   bien
wet   mouillé-e
What a pity!   Quel dommage!
what   quoi
What's new?   Quoi de neuf?
when   quand
where   où
whisky   le whisky
white   blanc, che
white wine   le vin blanc
Who knows?   Qui sait?

130

why   pourquoi
wide   large
widow   la veuve
widower   le veuf
wife   la femme
wind   le vent
window   la fenêtre
wine   le vin
wine steward   le sommelier
winter   l'hiver (m)
wish   l'envie (f)
with   avec
withdraw   retirer
witness   le témoin
woman   la femme
woods   le bois
work day   le jour ouvrable
work   le travail
work   travailler
wound   la blessure
wrist watch   la montre-bracelet
write   écrire

Y

year   l'an (m), l'année
yellow   jaune
yes   oui
yesterday   hier
You don't say!   C'est pas vrai!
you're welcome   de rien
young   jeune

Z

"zip" code   le code postale

131